PASSION FOR THE HUMAN SUBJECT

PASSION FOR THE HUMAN SUBJECT

A Psychoanalytical Approach Between Drives and Signifiers

Bernard Penot

KARNAC

First published in 2008 by
Karnac Books
118 Finchley Road
London NW3 5HT

Copyright © 2008 by Bernard Penot

The rights of Bernard Penot to be identified as the author of this work have been asserted in accordance with §§ 77 and 78 of the Copyright Design and Patents Act 1988.

Translated by Elizabeth Kelly.

All rights reserved. No part of this publication may be reproduced, stored in a retrieval system, or transmitted, in any form or by any means, electronic, mechanical, photocopying, recording, or otherwise, without the prior written permission of the publisher.

British Library Cataloguing in Publication Data

A C.I.P. for this book is available from the British Library

ISBN: 978–1–85575–586–4

Edited, designed, and produced by Communication Crafts

www.karnacbooks.com

CONTENTS

ABOUT THE AUTHOR   vii

Introduction   1

1   The drive circuit as generator of subjectivation   15

2   Oral drive functioning and subjection   29

3   "A Child Is Being Beaten":
    the three stages of the subjectivation of fantasy   42

4   The misfortunes of Sophie, or the *bad subject* to come   51

5   Adolescence of the Freudian subject   59

6   Foreclosure of signification and the suffering subject   75

7	The key role of the *phallus* signifier in the subjectivation of sexuality	93
8	Sublimation, latency, and subjectivation	106
9	Unexpected drive subjects in the session	131
10	The logical stages of subjectivation	150

| REFERENCES | 171 |
| INDEX | 177 |

ABOUT THE AUTHOR

Dr Bernard Penot is a psychiatrist (Paris, Salpêtrière, 1972), member of the Paris Psychoanalytical Society, and training analyst in the Paris Psychoanalytical Institute (1992); he was director of the *Cerep-Montsouris* day hospital for teenagers in Paris from 1988 to 2004; since 1996 he has been working as a training analyst in Istanbul.

His publications include:

Figures du déni—en deçà du négatif (Paris: Dunod, 1989; Toulouse: Erès, 2003); Portuguese edition (Brazil): *Figuras da Recusa: aquém do negativo* (Porto Alegre: Artes Medicas, 1992).

La passion du sujet freudien—entre pulsionnalité et signifiance (Toulouse: Erès, 2001); Portuguese edition (Brazil): *A Paixao do Sujeito Freudiano* (Rio de Janeiro: Companhia de Freud, 2005).

Dictionnaire International de Psychanalyse—with Alain de Mijolla (Paris: Calmann-Levy, 2002).

Introduction

> Freud did not go straight down that trail whose markers he has bequeathed to us. And so it may be that we are, as an effect of Freud's detours, clinging to a certain point in the evolution of his thinking, without being really aware of the contingent character it presents, like any effect of human history.
>
> Jacques Lacan, Seminar VIII: "The Ethics of Psychoanalysis"
> (1959–60, p. 106)

The condition of the human subject demands that he acquire his existence at the price of a real *passion*. And what, indeed, could inspire more *passion* than this ambiguous being, constantly trying to balance dynamically where nature and culture intersect?

The psychoanalytic approach launched by Freud a century ago has constantly posited as a structural fact the precarious position of human subjectivity. It conceives the latter as knocked off-centre, even torn apart, by the different logics emanating from the instances that make up the psychic apparatus. The most fundamental point of both the *topics* formalized successively by Freud is that the psychic apparatus is constituted of a structural heterogeneity, comprised of different systems, which are, in sum, strangers to each other—to the extent that what is pleasing to one, he says, could be displeasing to the other.

What Freud named the *Unconscious* in his first topic does indeed constitute a sort of *elsewhere* within each human being, an intimate stranger from whom emanates all those messages the psychoanalyst works to decipher through dreams, parapraxes, and symptoms. . . . In these, the *Unconscious* system finds its own way of expressing itself, according to rules different from those of conscious thought. The dream-work, for example, organizes "thing representations" in accordance with the principle of contiguity, condensation, and non-contradiction that Freud attributes to the primary thought process—so that we must decipher these clues as we would figurative signs in another language (like that of ideograms and rebuses).

Undoubtedly echoing Plato's famous myth of the cave, Freud says in the *Interpretation of Dreams* (1900a) that *unconscious complexes* are played out on "another stage" of representation than that of our waking psychic life.

For this structural heterogeneity within the human being, Freud's topics of the psychic apparatus offer models that engender, not a new psychology but, rather, as Feud himself emphasizes, a *meta*psychology.

An elsewhere within

The preposition *meta-* here connotes an off-centre conception of the psyche, and thus it breaks with the ego-centred psychologies that had been prevalent up to that time. The same prefix, *meta-*, occurs in the French *métèque*—meaning foreigner, related to the Greek *met'oikos*, which literally means something like an "elsewhere/house". So it would not be too far-fetched to characterize the Freudian Unconscious as a sort of stranger, a foreigner inside each one of us—a formulation that, though perhaps a little daring, essentially agrees with what Jean-Luc Donnet (1995) has called "operation meta".

However, the metapsychological revolution set in motion by Freud still wounds human self-esteem by attacking the ego-centred narcissistic image that man likes to have of himself. To this day, it still fuels a fundamental and continually reactivated *resistance* against psychoanalysis: on the one hand, from self-proclaimed "scientific" milieus (especially, alas, in the medical field) who try to discredit the specifically *subjective* aim of psychoanalytic research; and, on the other hand, from a certain philosophy that rejects the precariousness of a subjective condition submitted to unconscious determinism.

More insidiously, in our supposedly "post-Freudian" times, a *soft* form of anti-psychoanalysis often consists in designating as "psychoanalytic" practices that are in fact simple ego therapies, conducted according an approach that reverts to a psychological conception repudiating the *meta-* dimension; but such practices actually ignore the psychoanalytic approach, insofar as the latter is specifically defined as methodically listening to this stranger, this foreigner, this subjective *not-me* at work deep within the intimacy of everyone.

It takes a great dose of naïveté to be able to shout out, like one of our singers, "*Je suis moi!*" [I'm me!]. For what practicing psychoanalysis never stops showing us is more the irreducible antagonism between the narcissistic ego, in which we imagine ourselves coherent, constant—and even immortal!—and the uncertainties of that subject of desire and real inspiration whose living root springs from the stranger within oneself.

Helping patients to "work through" this, in order to put it into a *dialectic* form, is in the end the essential undertaking of any psychoanalytic treatment. This other, this intimate foreigner, who troubles and inspires us, whether perceived as a danger from within or as one coming from outside, dangerously mobilizes the forces of desire and thus tends to provoke hatred in the (narcissistic) ego. It is not surprising, therefore, that the totalitarian illusions and hasty simplifications of extreme rightist speech, which cultivate narcissistic unity (the illusion of race, for example), can only lead to a lamentable drying-up of creativity, because it is necessary for them to keep rejecting the living forces of inspiration. For the *fear of the stranger* is, in fact, equivalent to a fear of desire.

These primary defensive reactions re-emerge more than ever in our times, when a growing number of our fellow citizens are experiencing unemployment and exclusion and feel as though they have been deprived of the means for dealing with their own existential condition. This is all the more the case now that an objectifying discourse has spread its hegemony everywhere, when the ravages of an unfettered—supposedly "progressive"—free-market system are sweeping the world, and while such "scientific" techniques as surveys and polls are used systematically to evacuate any subject of socio-political responsibility. Would it, then, be unreasonable to think that the appearance of Freud's discoveries, at the dawn of the twentieth century—a century of totalitarianisms and epic destruction of men by their fellow men—was meant to provide a sort of *antidote* for totalitarian conceptions and reductive fundamentalisms?

In any case, it is a fact that Freud never succumbed to the siren song of Unitarian conceptual simplification, and that in spite of all (notably Jung), he held on to the non-unity of the psychic apparatus, the dissymmetry of the sexes, and, finally, to a fundamental dynamic duality in the drives. It is also this foreigner-in-the-house that Freud explored in his work on "The Uncanny" (1919h), which opens with a strict linguistic study of the fundamental ambiguity of the German term *heimlich*, showing how it plays continually on the interplay of meaning between the familiar/intimate and the strange.

The fact remains that this fundamental heterogeneity that psychoanalysis reveals to be at work within the human being tends to constitute both a treasure and a threat within. In the history of everyone's psychic development, the first *métèque*, the first intimate foreigner one meets, is none other than . . . one's father! It is upon this other that the so-called paternal metaphor (Lacan) must operate: the transforming displacement of libidinal investments originally placed in the maternal partner. This libidinal moving[1] constitutes an indispensable step in the development of every human subject.

But this subjective experience of heterogeneity will at the same time run up against the decisive ordeal of the *perception of the other gender*. Freud understood early in his work that, for the little boy, it is first and foremost a horror to discover that his mother has no penis. A lifetime of experience will not be enough to dispel the scandal of human beings' manifest dissimilarity, this element of radical—and anti-narcissistic—incompleteness that intimate relations with women will bear out: the penis can be missing, and irremediably so! We still see how *fundamentalisms* of every stripe strive to reduce the exchange between the sexes to the bare minimum necessary for procreation—undoubtedly because the essentially narcissistic source that animates their beliefs enjoins them to combat the unacceptable blow to *integrity* that is struck by human beings' incurable sexual differentiation—the first concretization of the "incompleteness of the symbolic" (Le Gaufey, 1991).

We must also take into consideration the basic fact that any procreation of a human being results from a *crossing between two lines* that are more or less matched, but necessarily heterogeneous (because incest must also be avoided!), an assemblage of relative strangers—a patchwork, one might say—stretching back as far as the eye can see.... In the end, is it not peculiar to the human subject that he is always engendered by *cross-breeding*? So that we may well wonder whether human beings produced by the process of *cloning* could ever be subjects, at least in our sense of the word....

Of course, the heterogeneity of generational lines will show more in cases marked by *transplantation*. But the fact remains that to each generation—more or less removed, more or less hybrid, more or less adopted—falls the task of continuing the manufacture of a history that can be shared and that gives an account of these assemblages and their more or less compatible (marriageable) meanings, so that the coexistence of the lines can be liveable. This necessary verbalization of existential elements, this mythmaking—*mythos* simply meant "speech" in ancient Greek—can give each generation the means of articulating in representable terms the different, more or less foreign roots of its existence.

The psychoanalytic process at work in a treatment is precisely a transforming work [*working through, perlaboration, Durcharbeitung*] on this intimate relation with what is heterogeneous in oneself. Thus it seems somewhat naïve to express this structural relation merely in terms of "frustration" and "conflict", as though it were based on misunderstandings that are fortuitous, transitory, and resolvable—when prolonged experience of the intimate frequentation of the stranger within oneself is precisely what we should require of anyone who intends to become a psychoanalyst.

Passivity–passivation

If subjective appropriation is the principal aim of psychoanalytic practice, it should be pointed out that the very notion of subjectivation is rooted in that of subjection—in other words, that subjectivity entails first a dimension of subjugation, of being submitted to something.

It implies that the very notion of "passivity"[2] must first be examined, insofar as it constitutes a real crossroads of the psychic dynamic. Indeed, its impact changes completely depending on whether one focuses more on its defensive, neutralizing aspect or on its fertile receptiveness. One can make oneself passive in order to cancel out one's involvement, to absent oneself from any exchange, particularly aggressive—the animal kingdom provides many illustrations of this tactic. This negative conception of passivity has been especially emphasized by authors of Kleinian inspiration. This is not the angle from which I will approach it within the framework of this book: I will, rather, treat *passivation* as constituting a decisive stage in the exercise of the drives, one that helps to accomplish the very process of *subjectivation*.

This term "passivation" was introduced by André Green in his 1980 work "Passions et destins des passions" ("Passions and their vicissitudes"), the title of which stresses its filial relation to Freud's "Instincts and Their Vicissitudes" (1915c). I, too, will use Freud's text as a starting point, for it contains the beginnings of an original, specifically psychoanalytic approach to the *subject function*: one that involves a *subject-agent* of drive exercise within the earliest interrelationships.

The *subject* thus conceived is, of course, distinctly different, by virtue of its primal character and possible unconsciousness, from the traditional subject of philosophers—whose degree of consciousness (as psychoanalysts are paid to know) offers no guarantees, since it might well involve a *false self* and *disavowal*. But the subject I am speaking of here, a subject of the drives, also cannot be placed within the "purely symbolic" register—as the purely grammatical subject to which Lacan's heritage is so generally, and wrong-headedly, reduced, since the Freudian perspective repudiates any unsubstantiated subject.

However, Lacan's own reliance on linguistics[3] led him very early to conceive of the subject as fundamentally *divided* from the start—notably between the subject of the *statement* (strictly and formally grammatical) and the subject of the *enunciation* (which sustains the implicit motivation of what has been said).

This fundamental duplicity of the subject (of speech and of act) is especially illustrated in the famous "Why?" of small children that adults strive, in vain, to answer. Take, for example, the following dialogue: the adult says: "It's nice outside"; the child asks, "Why?"; whereupon the adult tries to provide objective explanations that only lead to more compulsive repetitions of the "Why?" This is because the child's question is actually addressed not to the subject of the adult's statement, but to the subject of his implicit *enunciation*. Its true formulation would go something more like, "What's with you? What makes *you* tell *me* that *it* is nice?"

Let us note in passing the compound structure of the preceding sentence, with its three personal pronouns: we will be seeing this again in the arguments that follow (chapters 1, 3). We also see how the frame of mind it expresses—*paranoid*, in that it addresses the latent subject of the enunciation[4]—is akin to that of the psychoanalyst in the session.

Clinical work with subjectivation

The genesis of my interest in (my *passion* for) what determines true subjectivation—that is, drive-subjectivation—comes most of all from the margins of my practice—notably with *serious disorders of subjectivation in adolescence* (chapters 4, 5, 6). For if Freud's approach essentially involved using the pathological to shed light on the normal, one should expect that a psychoanalytic conception of the subject function may be developed from experience with deficiencies of this same function. This work springs from the observation that, for an analyst working with patients whose subject function has been "mortgaged" by an invalidating *alienation*, it can be heuristic and effective to create a dialectic between what can be designated as "functions of the ego" (integrative–defensive and fundamentally narcissistic) and what constitutes this "new subject" (Freud, 1915c), the *drive agent* of unconscious desire.

Psychopathology supplies various clinical scenarios according to which such a subject can appear to be mortgaged by an ego endowed with a kind of obstructing hypertrophy. Such is the case with the patients ruled by an *operative* thought mode (Smadja, 1998); but also with certain *obsessional neuroses* where the ego's mastery and need for control stifle subjectivation. Different forms of psychosis, or of pathologies referred to as conduct disorders, constitute still other ways of obliterating the subject of a desire. . . .

Lacan worked hard to make this egoistic alienation more explicit—he was carried along by the surrealist wave of the midcentury, while at the same time wishing to carry on what he considered to be decisive trailblazing by Freud. In his seminar "The Logic of Fantasy" (1966–67, unpublished), Lacan revisits Descartes's famous *cogito* to show how it comes to constitute a sort of *inverse* of the subject of the Unconscious dealt with by psychoanalysis. For what emerges from the metapsychological off-centring accomplished by Freud, with his "topics" making up the psychic apparatus, is, rather, as Lacan enjoyed formulating it: "I do not think there where I am" (unconsciously acting), and "I am not there where I think" (narcissistically)!

"There where I think I grasp myself in my narcissistic image, I am very far from the subject that is agent of my acts and promoter of my dreams." And it is precisely this distance between the conscious ego (that familiar narcissistic image of oneself) and the nascent subject of the drive exercise that requires the interminable effort at psychic binding [*Bindung*] to be endlessly redone: the always laborious cobbling together of a functional articulation between terms that are resistant to articulation. And from this perspective, we see very well how the "working through" that psychoanalytic treatment strives to encourage can never be considered finished—for the good reason that its terms will remain, structurally, strangers to one another, not speaking the same language.

And it is indeed an intimate and continuous frequentation of the stranger in oneself that should be required of anyone who intends to become a psychoanalyst for others.

Complexity of the "I"

The fact remains that Freud always insisted on gathering under the heading of the first-person singular *ich* an entire spectrum of functions, running from narcissistic blinding by which it can provoke defensive obstruction, to the key role of grasping a signifying bond that makes it the supposed ally of the psychoanalytic work. But to this day we can measure the theoretical difficulties that this composite character of Freud's *ich* has engendered—starting with the famous phrase *Wo es war, soll ich werden*, which the first French translations treated as referring to as *das Ich* [*le moi*], not to the first person [*je*] of the subject pronoun.

In fact, the *das Ich* (with capital I), the ego as instance, is essentially constructed out of elements of spatial representation (visual, cenesthesic) of one's own body. "*The ego is above all a corporeal ego*", Freud states (1923b); and this instance will mainly take on representative substance in the specular relation with the other (counterpart), and then in its identifications with successive partners. Overall, the ego is inscribed within the register Lacan called "imaginary", that of spatio-corporal representation. It is the only one of the three psychic instances of Freud's second topic that could be characterized, topologically, as being formed out of an introjected inside standing in opposition to a rejected outside (Freud, 1925h)—since the superego and the id surpass, to a certain extent, the very notion of the intrapsychic.

The instance that Freud calls the *superego*, obviously partly trans-individual and trans-generational, will form the boundary necessary for any communal conviviality. This superego also constitutes a limit figure, and I for one have suggested (Penot, 1995) that it be considered essentially *as an internal warning sign indicating the limit of the parent's love*, the threshold of parental tolerance.

A turning point in Freud's thinking was his revelation of what he chose to call *narcissism* (1914c), which made him conceive of the corporeal ego as a libidinal object for oneself. It is not so much the unconscious part of this ego but, rather, its narcissistic essence—that is, its dual characteristic of being formed in the specular relation, and of being fundamentally in the service of the pleasure principle—that led Freud to the theoretical necessity of envisioning a *beyond the pleasure principle* (1920g). And it is precisely in this that the subject function can be distinguished as not simply reducible to narcissism.

If we are to continue on this path, it seems to me that our theorization as psychoanalysts needs to take into consideration, as specifically as possible, and without mixing them up, the registers of the *real*, the *imaginary*, and the *symbolic*. In this regard, we should not hesitate to take advantage of what proves to be useful in the work of Jacques Lacan. I have decided to let myself be carried (*passivation oblige!*) by certain seminal Lacanian concepts, which tend to characterize as an essential pole of the psychic apparatus the subject of desire and inspiration coming from the id (see Figure 1 in Chapter 9). It should be understood that I have no intention here of discussing the whole of Lacan's contributions to psychoanalytic theory—especially as his thinking evolved considerably over thirty years of research (perhaps even more than Freud's did). I shall just try to use some conceptual tools he offers (*metaphorical* ones, it should be kept in mind) in order to understand better the essential symptoms of the suffering unconscious subject.

I attempt to show how the building-up of the subject function in the treatment, the subject of drive inspiration and not of narcissistic defence, is fundamentally the result of this conjunction of drive energy with meaning. This leads me to suggest that the subject be defined as *a drive agent caught up in a signifying relation.*

The first appearance of this subject takes place within the earliest mother–child relations, between the *real* of drives, on the one hand, and the *symbolic* charge of reactions (responses) coming from the mother. Such a conjunction is reinforced by the repeated exercise of getting something done to oneself, through both the constantly renewed exercise of drive energy and the always surprising interplay of signifying creativity.

But such subjectivating passivation can only be perceived as something "beyond the pleasure principle". This is certainly what Jacqueline Schaeffer (1997) illustrates when she speaks of "the defeat of the ego", which she sees as necessary in both sexes for achieving enjoyment beyond the mere pleasure of release. We may also refer to the work Marie-Christine Laznik-Penot has done on this issue (1990).

We know *a contrario* how Freud (1937d) designated "the horror of passivity" as the basic spring of the ego defences, insofar as the ego is in the service of control, of narcissistic integrity and the primacy of the pleasure principle.

The subject function, more specifically

My approach will be guided, therefore, by references somewhat different from those of Raymond Cahn in his report "Le sujet" ["The Subject"] to the 1991 Congrès des Psychanalystes de Langue Française (Cahn , 1991b). I congratulate him here for having tried to put forward what he called an "archaeology of the subject", and I recognized in his work many aspects of the treatments we carried on together for many years with seriously ill adolescents.

But the step I take here differs from his in that it intends to define the subject function much more narrowly. I shall not conceive of the subject as supposed to represent the *human person* as a whole, nor as the narcissistic image the latter can have of him/herself, still less as the reflexive notion of *self* which tends to designate an overall self-referential ("self-centred") function. The subject I am now trying to define psychoanalytically is not characterized by plenitude or naturalness, but seems, rather, to define itself as a *precarious function*, resulting from the human newborn's condition of prematuration, and therefore from the earliest drive transactions between the baby and its mother, including the mother's verbal and gestural responses.

This "condition of the subject" will be reiterated, throughout life, in various experiences of subjective interaction—that is, drive interaction with partners (implying their reciprocal passivation). Subjectivation arises from the interplay between drives and signifying responses, and not only *inter urinas et faeces*, as the Church Fathers said—and the subject's radical dividedness (incompleteness) derives from these very conditions.

Working as a psychoanalyst to help a patient establish better bonds between the different registers of his/her psyche does not imply giving in to unifying, globalizing, simplifying, or isolating illusions but, rather, requires that we never lose sight of the heterogeneity (including the irremediable differentiation of the sexes), which is just what Freud's metapsychology introduced. Thus the ordeal of *otherness*—with regard to the sex we don't have, the language we don't speak, the means we don't possess—is indispensable in affirming a subjectivity.

This being said, I shall refrain from beginning (as is usual) with some dictionary definitions of the term *subject*. I would instead emphasize that the subject-in-the-psychoanalytic-sense that I am trying to approach here is still awaiting definition, that it is a concept in gestation. I shall, nevertheless, try to bring together some elements of a definition at the end of chapter 9.

In the subsequent chapters I shall attempt the following:

Starting with an examination (chapter 1) of the use of the word "subject" in Freud's "Instincts [Drives] and Their Vicissitudes" (1915c), I go on to give a first illustration of a basic subjective problematic, using the treatment of a bulimic patient (chapter 2).

I continue to study (chapter 3) the key role passivation plays in the *construction of fantasy*, with reference to "A Child Is Being Beaten" (Freud, 1919e).

After this, I give some examples of borderline adolescents and the institutional treatment of their defective subjectivation (chapters 4, 5, 6).

From there, I go on to provide a better definition of the key notion of *signifier*, using as an example the functional vicissitudes of the mental representation of the phallus (chapter 7).

After this, I re-examine how *sublimation* (chapter 8) can help towards a better grasp of the drive subject.

I then recount (chapter 9) some moments of a psychoanalytic session wherein the patient could benefit, in her drive life, from submitting (passivating) herself to the emergence of some key signifiers.

I conclude (chapter 10) with a re-examination of time (the discontinuity of "scansion" and deferred action) as a factor in the basic subjectivating experience between interacting subjects.

Notes

1. In present-day Greece, the word *metaphorai* can be seen on removal vans!

2. This was the theme of the Congrès des Psychanalystes de Langue Française held in Paris in May 1999, entitled "Enjeux de la passivité" [The Stakes of Passivity], where I gave a report, "La passion du sujet, entre pulsionnalité et signifiance" [Passion for the subject, between drives and signifiers] (Penot, 1999), which gave rise, in large part, to this book.

3. This report owes much to the work done in our seminar on "Lacan Reading Freud", which was conducted for several years at the Institut de Psychanalyse, rue Saint-Jacques, Paris, with the participation of (among others) Sylvie Faure, Alain Fine, Marie-Eugénie Jullian, and Georges Pragier, to whom I give my warmest thanks.

4. The French comedian Coluche captured this paranoid dimension very well when, in a stand-up routine about a disastrous picnic, he griped, *"I even thought it was gonna rain—it's such a dumb-ass!"* We laugh at how much of the consistency of the real such an impersonal "it" can have—like the id (and, in a sense, like God . . .). [This impression is even stronger in French, where the pronoun *il* can mean both "it" and "he"].

CHAPTER ONE

The drive circuit as generator of subjectivation

> One day we're going to have to accept that the most subversive part of Freud's thought is that it upsets the theory of subjectivity by placing at its origin the myth of the drive, by making the subject into the subject of the drive . . . at times leading the drive, at other times being lead by it.
>
> André Green (1989)

If Freud generally avoided the use of the term "subject" in his work, it is probably because he was wary of its established usage in philosophy to designate a supposedly pre-eminent instance of the psyche—that very same conscious ego that has been dethroned by Freud's attempt at decentralizing the psychic apparatus, which is the foundation of his metapsychology.

There is, however, one remarkable exception to Freud's avoidance of this term. In "Instincts[1] and Their Vicissitudes" (Freud, 1915c), he repeatedly and systematically refers to the notion of *subject* when evoking a certain kind of destiny (vicissitude) of basic pairs of drives: that in which the *turning around upon oneself* (upon one's own body) combines with *reversal into its opposite*. This is a reversal of the *aim* of the drive—that is, the satisfaction sought in an active or a passive way. Freud also mentions here another kind of reversal, of *content*, found in the single instance of the transformation of love into hate—which he will later examine separately.

Let us see at what point in this key text Freud needs to have recourse to the notion of *subject*. It is precisely when he is determined to describe this ordinary destiny of basic drive pairs, the combination of the two above-mentioned complementary movements: the *turning around* of drive activity onto one's own body, and the *reversal* of an *active* mode of satisfaction into a *passive* one (to get oneself looked at, to get oneself taken in hand). It is in describing this reversal of satisfaction into a passive mode that Freud introduces the presence of a *subject*. But it is striking that he places this *"new subject"*, as he calls it, outside the own-person (an *"extraneous subject"*), the agent of a gaze or of his handling. The subject within the *own-person* is then supposed to be in a sort of suspension.

Freud proposes to illustrate this by means of a first antagonistic drive pair that he calls *sadomasochistic*—for he seems unable to avoid using the psychiatric terminology of perversions when dealing with basic instinctual life. He evokes the first activity of the newborn: a violence against whatever is within his reach, which is objectively sadistic but innocent insofar as its degree of subjectivation is minimal; he notes that "the infliction of pain plays no part among the original purposive actions [of the drive]". Afterwards, the child's "sadism" tends to take his own body as an object, a practice that Freud qualifies as *auto-erotic*. Freud subsequently describes a third phase where the drive seeks satisfaction in a passive mode for which he coins the term *masochistic*. "An extraneous person is once more sought as object; this person, in consequence of the alteration which has taken place in the instinctual [drive] aim, has to take over the role of the subject" (p. 127).

This is the first appearance of the term *subject*, by which Freud clearly intends to designate the outside *agent* of a drive activity, a sadistic one in this particular instance, which strives to satisfy the masochistic demand of the person. Strachey remarks in a footnote what he calls a "confusion in the use of the word *subject*".[2] "As a rule", he says, "*subject* and *object* are used respectively for the person in whom an instinct . . . originates, and the person or thing to which it is directed. . . . Here, however, *subject* seems to be used for the person who plays the active part in the relationship—the agent [of drive]" (p. 127, fn). Freud, considering at that time an "original sadism", goes on to speak of a *"passive ego [Ich]"*—he will even speak of an *"own-object"*—giving in fantasy [sic] to *"the extraneous subject"* the sadistic position that he (ego) had first occupied.

At this point in the development of his thinking, Freud conceived of this passive-masochistic attitude as secondary—that is, as resulting from the *turning around/reversal* of the original sadistic impulse. He says: "A primary masochism, not derived from sadism in the manner I have described, seems not to be met with" (p. 128). But in later works about masochism (1924c), Freud expresses what he calls "an opposite view". In sum, we can see that Freud's three phases of drive activity reprise the three classical grammatical moods of verb conjugation: active, reflexive, and passive.

He then invites the reader to consider a second pair of opposing drives: the one whose goal, he says, is "to look and to display oneself", which, he immediately adds, would become *scopophilia* and *exhibitionism* in the language of perversions.

In his description of the *turning around/reversal* destiny of this new drive pair, Freud once more employs the term *subject* in speaking of the third phase, when there is a passivation of the goal—the satisfaction of being looked at:

> Here again, we may postulate the same stages as in the previous instance:—(a) Looking as an activity directed towards an extraneous object. (b) Giving up of the object and turning of the scopophilic instinct [drive] towards a part of [one's] own body; with this, transformation to passivity and setting up of a new aim—that of being looked at. (c) Introduction of a new subject to whom one displays oneself in order to be looked at by him. [1915c, p. 129]

Once again, Freud uses the term subject to designate the agent of an external gaze upon oneself.

I think three considerations can be derived from the functional schema Freud proposes through these two basic drive pairs.

1. First, both illustrate in a striking way an essential characteristic of drive: that its exercise is always *active* by nature (drive is "a

piece of activity", he says) even when its goal is passive satisfaction (to be looked at, to be handled). Freud's formula *"one displays oneself"* expresses very well this idea of implicit activity; and I think that the English formulation, *to get something done to oneself*, also captures the active nature of such a search for passive satisfaction—and designates by the same token the so-called *feminine position* in both sexes.

These considerations should help to counter Strachey's above-mentioned objections (and in a footnote). Freud shows an external *subject* that must satisfy the own-person's drive activity when its aim is a passive satisfaction. He thus shows how this so-called "passive" moment of drive vicissitude plays a decisive role in the new person's subjective appropriation. But beyond this, it leads us to consider that no *subject* can be constituted alone at any moment.

Drive interaction and its subjectivating function implies the participation of at least two *subjects*. I would say that it is fundamentally and from the beginning an *intersubjective* experience and, as such, necessarily implies a *third referential term*.

It is to the credit of André Green (1980) that he was able to promote this idea of drive *passivation*, which plays a key role in the process of genuine *subjectivation*. In fact, these two terms are neologisms, in French as well as in English. But their interest is that each one can be coupled with another more usual, less ambiguous, word connoting passivity, giving the pairs *passivity/passivation* and *subjection/subjectivation*. The terms of each pair are related but not synonymous, since the more usual words connote passivity, while their cognate neologisms dynamically express how drive activity may be directed towards passive satisfaction. Thus in the first pair, *passivity/passivation*, the second term does not express pure passivity but, more specifically, how drive *activity* can be directed towards a passive goal; while in the second pair, *subjection/subjectivation*, the second term implies a process of appropriation of the drive movement (whereas subjection connotes dispossession), a way of assuming and experiencing the drive activity as one's own—a movement accomplishing, in sum, the opposite of rejection or *disavowal* (Penot, 1998). From this perspective—a very fertile one in my opinion—it may be seen that the Freudian subject must proceed from the drive interplay, lest it be merely a *false self* or a defensive reaction formation.

2. But we must note that, in the two examples he gives, Freud starts by locating the subject *outside*: it is an *extraneous person*, he says, outside one's own-person. This external subject, agent of the activity of looking at or taking in hand, clearly corresponds here to something other than what is conventionally referred to as an *object* of the child's drive activity. Freud even speaks at this point of the "*giving up of the object*". It is striking that he places what he calls a "*new subject*" outside the physical person, as the agent of a gaze upon the latter or the agent of his handling—the subject within the person itself apparently being at that moment in a sort of suspension.

Already, in his "Project for a Scientific Psychology" (1950 [1895]), Freud had evoked the primordial function of aiding the newborn, performed by a person he calls (in the style of the gospels) the *neighbour* [*Nebenmensch*], the one who accepts to be the agent of the maternal function.

3. The question remains: which of the three phases of drive activity (active, reflexive, passive) comes first? We saw that in "Instincts and Their Vicissitudes", Freud emphasizes his own conviction that "it can hardly be doubted that the active aim appears before the passive, the looking precedes being looked at". (p. 129)

In his later work, however, Freud's convictions on this issue would vacillate. Most notably, he was to argue the opposite opinion, nine years later, in "The Economical Problem of Masochism" (1924c), where he presents primary masochism as a consequence of the condition of the human infant's prematurity. Freud does not fail to point out this change of opinion in a footnote to a new edition (in 1924) of "Instincts and Their Vicissitudes" (1915c). Nevertheless, this remarkable theoretical fluctuation concerning the primacy of sadism, or masochism, or of auto-eroticism, appears to me to be in itself *symptomatic*: an indication of the pivotal role these reversals of position in drive activity can have in the process of subjectivation. This leads one to consider that the degree and richness of a person's subjectivation may be determined by his/her ability to experience a smooth passage from one position to another, to develop subjective enjoyment within an exchange that is not merely a search for release.

The drive circuit

It is precisely in view of this crucial question that Jacques Lacan undertook, beginning in the mid-1950s, his examination of Freud's work. Lacan's seminar "The Partial Drive and Its Circuit" (1964) can shed some light on this issue. He first argues that any drive is *sexual* (even if it belongs to the register of orality or anality) and, moreover, necessarily *partial* (even if it is genital), in view of sexuality's biological end: procreation. Having said this, he insists on using Freud's text to show the kind of *"back and forth"* by which each drive couple tends to take shape following a three-stage path.

Here, Lacan has the simple idea of representing the drive's accomplishment as making a *circuit*, a loop, wherein the three positional modes argued by Freud succeed each other, forming a retroactive trajectory going around the incidental object that is its obscure aim (the lost first object). What then becomes clear for Lacan is that the satisfaction of the drive will reside more in the degree of accomplishment of this loop, the richness of its circuit, than in any attempt to actually possess or master the object itself. This reminds me of what the Greek poet Cavafy says of the Odyssey in his poem "Ithaka":

Ithaka gave you the beautiful voyage . . .
it has nothing else to give you.

Is this not the same idea—of an object serving as a pretext, as the cause of an adventure—that lies behind the many cycles of the Grail quest? That the journey itself is the aim. . . .

Lacan considers that it is not as it grasps its incidental (manifest) object that any drive can be satisfied; indeed, it is when the object is in its grasp that the drive learns that satisfaction cannot be derived from the object, because "no object of need can satisfy drive". What drive seeks above all is something from the primal other. This is particularly true of the oral drive: "The mouth opening up in the register of drive (activity)", say Lacan, "is not going to be satisfied with food". This is what we keep learning from bulimic patients: no food ever gives satisfaction in the drive quest, which is always aiming for the *lost–lacking object.*

But, one might ask, what primordial lost (or failed) satisfaction is the bulimic's oral drive indefinitely in quest of? I would say it is probably seeking to be allowed to experience the satisfaction of feeling delectable, as an infant, in the eyes of the mother, a way of satisfying the drive for oral satisfaction in a passive mode, without being destroyed by it. In other words, it seeks to be in a position of *oral passivation* in relation its object. But the danger of assuming the passive position of object of the mother's oral drive, first experienced in infancy, can induce a defensive exercise of oral drive activity, lowering the goal for satisfaction to the level of the de-metaphorized object of alimentary need.

Bulimic and anorexic patients usually illustrate this kind of failure to experience a genuine, enriching process of oral drive passivation—and, of course, the way this process can make the experience of romantic love more dynamic. The treatment of Vera (chapter 2) seems to me to exemplify this. Vera could gain a certain freedom and enrich her capacities for exchange through the re-actualization, in the transference relationship, of her repetitive, defensive need to *reject* a form of oral dependence on her object that she experienced as degrading and dehumanizing. To overcome this blockage, she had to (re)experience the *reversibility* of active–passive interplay within the analytic exchange, and this required her analyst to take his turn at being *passivated*.[3]

Lacan goes on to say: "If thanks to the introduction of the other, the structure of the drive appears [along with its representability], it is really completed only in its reversed form, in its return form."

This is particularly evident in the case of exhibitionism where "that which is the aim of the subject (agent of drive) is what is realized in the other"—while the latter is looking.

Reconsidering the place of *auto-eroticism* in the drive circuit, Lacan emphasizes the necessary localization in one's own body of the beginning and end of drive. "Everything that Freud spells out", Lacan says, "about partial drives shows us the circular ... movement of the pressure, which goes out through the erogenous border [the source] and returns to it as its [auto-erotic] target, after having gone around something I call object little a".

But what follows is more surprising. Lacan concludes: "I would argue that it is through this [the accomplishment of the drive circuit] that the subject will reach what is, properly speaking, the dimension of the great Other." Here he means, of course, the *symbolic great Other*, which he usually defines as *the "place" of the set of signifiers that contribute to the determination of the subject*. However, Lacan makes clear at this point that this must also be a real other, the person who fulfils the parental function at the beginning of life.

The Other of the drive

Marie-Christine Laznik-Penot (1993) was the first to call attention, in Lacan's 1962–63 seminar (as yet unpublished), to the surprising conjunction between the symbolic big Other and the real parent at the origin of life. This occurs at the very place where what Freud calls the *new subject*—the external agent of the drive—will appear. This conjunction between real primordial parent and symbolic big Other has been generally neglected, if not rejected outright, in specifically Lacanian circles, though Jean Laplanche (1970, 1989) did touch upon it in a certain way when he gave a fundamental place to his "seduction theory" at the very beginning of psychic development.

Laznik-Penot's particular experience in treating small autistic children and their parents confronted her with the primary condition of drive exchange for any subjectivation. She came to consider that while the autistic child without language does have something that takes the place of an *ego*, an "ego-machine", he or she still does not have access to what I would define here as a *subject function*, precisely because he/she could not complete the drive circuit in his/her relation with his/her first parental partner.

Any child is marked by his/her first interactions with his/her mother; these organize the decisive and very *real* differentiation of the child's erogenous zones, the way he/she will be able to invest his/her corporal orifices, which are the sources of the drive. From then on, it is in the repeated accomplishment of the drive circuit, through the passive reversal of the mode of satisfaction, that the nascent subject will *let him/herself* receive from the parental partner a decisive *signifying imprint* which will serve him/her as a personal structure. In sum, it is as if the concrete exercise of the drive coming from the body had to combine repeatedly, from the very beginning, with significations giving a *symbolic* dimension to the exchange with the parental other, in order that true subjectivity might be established and develop in the child.

The very process of psychoanalytic treatment may be viewed from this angle, insofar as subjectivating appropriation is supposed to occur through the repeated exercise of various registers of passivation—getting heard, getting interpreted (getting analysed, as we say)—which open one up to a growing capacity for experiencing oneself as a subject of one's own drive activity (*Wo Es war, soll Ich werden*).

An essential point here is that any drive, as it accomplishes its circuit, will seek out something in the (parental) Other that must *answer* every time (see the case of Sophie, chapter 4).

Lacan concludes: "And the subject will be born insofar as, in the place of the Other, the signifier emerges—in other words, a signifying piece of a [parental] response to the [child's] drive overtures."

Thus, in a clear break with *naturalistic* conceptions of the subject within the psychoanalytic movement (notably, the first Kleinian approach), Lacan considers the drive movement at its origin—before it has been able to get a response from the Other—as not in itself containing any subject, as *"acephalic"*, he says. He thus emphasizes that symbolic signification is not *endogenous*, not an intrinsic property of the drive movement issuing from the body.

It is the response of the parental Other that will cause something of a *subject* to take form in the physical person of the child— as was revealed, in fact, two centuries ago, by the observation of "wild children" who had been raised by animals. In every experience of the accomplishment of the drive trajectory, what returns from the other, the parental message-signal (mainly unconscious), will attach a decisive indication (e.g., pleasure/displeasure) to the direct sensorial experience of the nascent subject.

The *subjection/subjectivation* pair will then take on all of its ambiguity, and even ambivalence, through a variety of possibilities for *getting something done to oneself*: getting seen, getting heard, getting eaten up by others, and of course, from the first day of school to our present working life, getting the shit bugged out of oneself. . . .

This shows how crucial is the capacity of the parental primordial partner to derive enough pleasure from *playing* while occupying a variety of drive positions *vis-à-vis* the child. An unvarying (defensive) parental attitude—of control, for example—tends to produce specific pathologies of subjectivation, in particular anorexia and bulimia.

In addition, the circular schema Lacan that proposes to represent the complete fulfilment of the drive trajectory has the advantage of overcoming the insoluble problem of figuring out what comes first—active or passive aim, sadism or masochism, looking or getting looked at. It also moves beyond Freud's strange and persistent representation of a complete auto-eroticism supposedly present at the life's origin (*primary narcissism*), a notion that, in addition to fostering a naturalistic vision of development, contradicts Freud's own knowledge that the fetus is actually in a state of symbiosis, and that one has to include with the infant's "psychical system . . . the care it receives from its mother" (Freud, 1911c [1910]).

A libidinal motor

I would suggest that we envision the Lacanian model of the drive circuit as a sort of *motor* whose energetic back-and-forth movement would be produced by the continuous succession of three stages: active, passive, and auto-erotic. Freud might have liked such a thermodynamic metaphor. The dynamic model of the running motor also makes it easier for us to retain Freud's surprising conviction about the *constancy* of drive (piston) pressure. In any case, it seems to me that the static notion of *poles*, and even of *positions*, is perhaps better suited for representing pathological forms of the dysfunction or lack of accomplishment of the drive circuit: when it is stuck in an unvarying position (this sort of blockage defines the *perverse* position, as opposed to the merely *erotic* one).

As an example of such pathologies, we may cite those cases characterized by frenzied activity: patients that French colleagues of the Paris Psychosomatic School have called "volunteer galley slaves" (Szwec, 1998) and others whose activities are mainly aimed at self-calming; or many other pathetic cases whose drive activity has been polarized from the beginning when it was pressed into the therapeutic service of parents needing constant reparation; and of course those who are indefinitely blocked into a passive-masochistic attitude (which is a failure of genuine passivation).

Both compulsive hyperactivity and withdrawal into passivity can be considered as expressing an inaptitude for the process of passivation I am talking about here. They can be considered as life-long *painkilling postures* adopted in order to avoid suffering too much from the primal helplessness (the Freudian *Hilflosigkeit*), exacerbated by the absence of adequate parental response within their earliest exchanges. In the normal back-and-forth of accomplished drive life, where the circuit is sufficiently elaborated through its different phases, each protagonist takes a turn at being an *object* for the other, and incidentally for him/herself. *Thus a decisive ability of any mother is to be able to let herself become an object*—an oral one, in the first instance.

The three-stage motor of the drive is obviously fuelled by the *libido*; but I think it is important to consider that this energetic fuel for the drive circuit actually has a double origin. There is, of course, the libido produced by one's own body (as we know, Freud envisions drive as a limit concept between soma and psyche). This same libidinal energy can come to be invested either within the drive circuit proper, as it is conceived of here, or within the narcissistic investment that follows from what Lacan (1949, p. 75) calls the "mirror stage", the perceptive experience of the overall ego and of the other. But in any case, the libidinal energy coming from the child's own body must meet with libidinal investment coming from the parental partner. In chapter 8 we return to the crucial importance of this parental investment and the characteristics it can have.

This leads us to emphasize that the primary *experience of satisfaction*, on which the first acquisitions of psychic development are founded, must itself be seen as twofold, the satisfaction of bodily needs necessarily interacting with the reception of signals of satisfaction coming from the parental partner. We are reminded of the possible early impact of signals of maternal phobia, which can go so far as to cause psychosis in a baby. The conjunction of these two experiential references guide and reinforce the process of subjectivation, providing it with the charge of investment necessary for life—and this long before the ego is sufficiently developed to face its global image, in what Lacan called the *mirror stage* (1936). I would add that it will be the job of the superego to re-present the *limit* of this parental cooperation.

One interest of these considerations would be to remind psychoanalysts that they must be ready, in many treatments, to tolerate asymmetry and even sometimes a real lack of proportion within the *transference relationship*, insofar as the patient needs to relive, by regression, something of the failure of his/her earliest exchanges. In other words, analysts must be prepared to assume the role of the original big Other in their patient's eyes—without of course actually believing themselves to be that!

D. W. Winnicott can be considered a pioneer in the fearless acceptance of such a position. He was the first to explicate, in his cool-headed way, the disproportion that can arise with certain patients and the importance of the analyst's ability to accept and go along with it. In this he may perhaps be seen, to some extent, as an heir to Sándor Ferenczi's less fortunate efforts.

We may take as an example the case of a male patient who had been through a number of treatments (Winnicott, 1971a), and to whom Winnicott did not hesitate to declare: "I am listening to a girl. I know perfectly well that you are a man but I am listening to a girl, and I am talking to a girl. I am telling this girl: 'you are talking about penis envy.'" He remarks: "It has been pointed out to me that my interpretation . . . could be thought of as related to playing, and as far as possible removed from authoritative interpretation that is next door to indoctrination." When, after a pause, the patient reacts by saying: "If I were to tell someone about this girl I would be called mad", Winnicott is surprised to hear himself reply: "It is *I* who see the girl and hear a girl talking, when actually there is a man on my couch. The mad person is *myself*" (Winnicott, 1971a, pp. 73–74). He thinks that "his" madness may have enabled the patient to see himself as a girl—but from the position of the analyst. He constructs the hypothesis that the mother (now deceased) had at first "seen" the patient as a baby girl, so that the man had to fit into his mother's idea that as a baby "he would be and was a girl". The patient had to organize his defences according to this "information" (he was the second child in his family, the first being a boy); but it was the madness of the mother who saw a boy where there was a girl—and this is what has been restored and re-established when the analyst states: "The mad person is myself."

Winnicott emphasizes that this has nothing to do with homosexuality. I personally believe that Winnicott did not think that it had to do with the analyst's own reality either but ought, rather, to be considered as a kind of *transference phenomenon*, re-actualizing something of the primal maternal gaze upon the patient—a *real* (perceptual) imprint left in his psyche before it could organize any fantasy representation.

I would add that, in this case, what must first be relived and then overcome is a kind of *community of disavowal* (Fain, 1982), between mother and child, that has been transferred into the analytic situation—a parental "madness" that evidently remained as an early perceptive imprint on the patient's experience. Such an imprint belongs to the psychic category Lacan calls the *real*, and would therefore predate the establishment of fantasy in the patient and the overall integration of his ego. It must acquire some (imaginary) *figurability* and (symbolic) *signification* if it is to constitute what Freud calls *psychic reality*—that is, an organized and representable fantasy scenario.

I now present, in chapter 2, the case of Vera, a young bulimic patient, which seems illustrative of this. Vera's drive activity was probably marked from the beginning by a serious, handicapping distortion in the exchange with her maternal other, and her subjective suffering could only be analysed by the repetition of it within the transference relation, where it took the form of a genuine impasse, an invalidating short-circuit. The mere recognition of this impasse as it was experienced in the analysis helped to open up new possibilities of subjectivation for Vera.

Notes

1. Strachey's choice of the term "instinct" to translate Freud's term "*Trieb*" has been criticized, because Freud's theorization of human *Trieb* clearly produced a new concept (a frontier concept) that, with its parameters of *pressure, aim, object, and source,* has little to do with instinctual *montages* in animals and appears to be more specific to human beings. Thus, the English term "drive" seems a much more adequate translation of "*Trieb*".

2. Strachey is obviously attached to a systematic use of the terms *subject* and *object* within a univocal polarity in which the *subject* is always supposed to correspond to the own-person. It is thus striking to see how, in his translation, he does not strictly follow Freud's use of the term *Subjekt*; he confusingly uses the English word *subject* three times when Freud does not, speaking of: "*the subject's own self*" (1915c, pp. 126, 127) and the "*subject's own body*" (p. 129). This makes it difficult to follow in English Freud's revolutionary idea of a necessary "time" during which an external drive agent, thus designated as *subject*, must be "put in place", outside, by the own-person to satisfy his drive aim of being treated as an object.

3. O. Renik gave striking clinical illustrations of this in, notably, "Affective Self-disclosure by the Analyst" (2000); I regret, however, that his theorization does not do justice to the whole *transferential* dimension.

CHAPTER TWO

Oral drive functioning and subjection

A young woman, whom I will call Vera, was afflicted with an oral drive destiny that took the form of bulimic episodes: an auto-erotic short-circuiting, no doubt aimed at staving off some unbearable subjective suffering. Any search for satisfaction in a passive mode seemed only to precipitate her into unconditional and degrading dependency. I came to suppose (in the sense of *constructions* in analysis) that a strong need for control on the part of her mother—a horror of passivation in the latter—might have given their drive exchanges a destructive character from the outset, mortgaging the development of Vera's oral libido. This patient had come to exercise her oral drive activity in a defensive way (autistically), falsely battening it down over the de-metaphorized object of alimentary need. Unable to access a reversibility in her partner (other) that would allow for a more subjectively enriching drive trajectory, she seemed to have maintained herself in a form of restrictive submission in relation to her first drive interactions.

With a patient of this type, the analyst will inevitably have to deal with the paradox of mutual *passivation*. For he or she must indeed start with the primary alienating submission (the passivity endured in relation to the mother) in order to find the dynamic of *turnings-around* and *reversals* (see chapter 1) that could lead to subjectivating appropriation. In this treatment, we will see that actualization, in the transference, of her rejection of dependency will enable this patient to free herself from it in a lasting way.

Vera's treatment

Vera was referred to me by her general practitioner for an analysis.[1] Vera first developed troubling bulimic symptoms in late adolescence, after ending her relationship with a young man who, she said, had been treating her "oddly". Their relationship lasted four years, until she was 20 years old. During their time together, this boy, who was very unsure of himself, became more and more demanding of total (and non-reciprocal) submission from her. She had to be completely "self-effacing" and to act as though she had "no hold on him". She says that she came to believe "it was impossible to go on living that way" and broke up with him.

She tells me that over the next four years she had a relationship with a very energetic and athletic boy, who had her parents' approval and who said he wanted to "rehabilitate" her! He manipulated her, stalked her, and seemed to want to put her through a sort of training programme. It now seems to her that she was "afraid of him". Her fear of him made her revert to anorectic behaviour. which, in retrospect, she interprets as an attempt to "inspire pity" in her boyfriend so that he would give up his demands. Vera likens the behaviour of this second boyfriend to her mother's, leading me to suppose that her mother's need for control—the mother's horror of passivity—could have given a destructive character to their drive exchange from the start.

In fact, the beginning of her therapy would show me that any satisfaction in a passive mode could only precipitate Vera into a state of unconditional and degrading dependence. So I began to suspect that, as her analyst, I would inevitably be caught up with her in the paradox of the dynamic pairing of *subjection/subjectivation*—in that decisive moment where true passivation must get past the appearance of dreaded passivity in order to experience the dynamic process of subjective appropriation. I think it is the path everyone must take in order to overcome an alienating submission to the parental partner.

At the time of our first interviews, Vera is 27 years old. She is in the process of breaking up with a third boyfriend, who is very shy and who, she complains, does not make her happy. She has again turned to bulimic compulsions that drive her to induce vomiting and that leave her feeling distressed and empty.

She works as an executive secretary and says that she is ready and able pay for three sessions per week; she can envisage lying down on the couch.

During the first year of her treatment, she shows a capacity for psychoanalytic *working through*, mainly with regard to the relationship that she had as a child with her mother, whom she leads me to imagine as very domineering and abusive. The mother was a homemaker from a rather traditional bourgeois family. According to Vera, this mother was possessive and quick-tempered towards her, exercising a sort of jealous domination over her. When Vera reached puberty at age 13, her mother began violently to accuse her of trying to "attract" her parents' friends.

Vera had learned to exercise her oral drive activity in a defensive manner, avoiding any significant response from her partners in love and lowering her goal for satisfaction to the de-metaphorized object of alimentary need. It is through the re-actualization in the transference of her rejection of oral dependence *vis-à-vis* her object that she will be able to gain a certain freedom and enrich her capacities for exchange.

Vera describes her father, an engineer, as a studious, retiring man, fond of old books, who seems to have abdicated all authority at home. Vera is the oldest of three children; she has a sister a year and a half younger, and a brother three years younger with whom the mother is said to be very indulgent.

"With Mom", she says, "I had to be . . . hmmm, just like YOU are here! I always had to listen to her. She talked about herself all the time. It's always been like that." We can note already how Vera spontaneously likens herself to her mother (as though she were mirroring her).

As a patient, she shows a kind of zeal that consists, among other things, in never allowing an instant of silence. In a few months, her bulimic symptoms disappear; she develops auto-erotic aptitudes, evident in her growing attention to her physical appearance and a new-found capacity for making herself quite attractive. She informs me that she has entered into a romantic relationship with a young executive at her place of work. She speaks as though she is finally happy with a man, so much so that they plan to get married at the end of the year. I am thinking that this newfound aptitude derives from a transference effect (fixation of the devouring danger upon myself), and I keep waiting to see what will happen next . . .

As might be expected, Vera's mother then tries to take over the wedding preparations, investing all her self-esteem in them, and Vera has to struggle hard against this new threat of being mastered and dispossessed (subjection). After a weekend at her parents' house, Vera tells me that she had a brief attack of bulimia on Sunday night. She is astonished at this *"return"*—*"just when things were going so well for me"*. This setback leads her to apply to herself, not without humour, the old joke about a madman who has supposedly been cured of his belief that he is a grain of wheat. He is released from the insane asylum, but he flees in terror at the sight of some chickens, saying: "I know I am not a grain of wheat, but maybe they don't know it! . . ." Vera knows she is better—but as for others (especially her mother), maybe they don't know it! . . .

Through associations, she brings up a painful memory from her childhood: her mother would quite often simply forget to come to get her at elementary school. This gave her a terrible feeling of having been dropped by her mother, and she would cry inconsolably. She still cries when she recalls it.

I try to call her attention to the apparent difference between the kind of sorrow she is talking about here and the kind she had been telling me about up till now: the one that would arise when her mother was bringing her back from ballet class. Her mother had made a big emotional investment in this daily activity—she had even managed to become a kind of secretary at the dance school. Their return together invariably left little Vera in tears, crushed by her mother's criticisms and remonstrances.

I point out that the cause of distress she has just evoked seems different from another one she has been talking about up till now, which used to occur when he mother was driving her home from dance class. Her mother had a huge investment in these dance lessons, and she had even managed to take on secretarial duties for the dance school, so that she could be present during all her daughter's lessons! Vera says that during the ride home she invariably burst into tears, as her mother criticized and castigated her. So she has evoked two apparently opposed sets of circumstances that would trigger her sorrow. She comments meekly on my remark (in her usual way), saying that her mother's treatment of her was in fact characterized by a kind of *"alternation"* between dropping her and controlling (mastering) her. In the latter case, she says she felt her mother was trying to "devour" her. I am struck by this crude evocation of an oral-drive interplay between mother and daughter.

At the same time, Vera remarks, her mother always seemed preoccupied with "people more interesting than I was"—as much as when she was heaping criticism upon her daughter, as when she forgot it was time to get her at school. *"Ah! How I hated her then, you can't imagine. She made fun of me. She never honoured schedules"*, Vera adds.

—I say: "And maybe you felt that she wasn't honouring you, that she was showing you a lack of consideration for your person?"

—*"I think it is something like that, because, at the time, I had a terrible desire to punish Mom . . . by hurting myself. I fantasized about being in an accident in the street. Hey! That must also be an aim of my anorexia and even my bulimia. . . . Anyway, I had to submit, to remain at her mercy. I didn't at all consider myself as an independent person."*

—I say that I am asking myself: "would walking home peacefully by yourself not have constituted a greater violence against your mother than being in an accident?"

—*"Our house wasn't far from the school, and I knew the way; but I didn't get a house key until I was 14. Ah! How I hated her then, you can't imagine. And she made fun of me."*

—I insist: "Maybe going home by yourself, like other children, would have inflicted something worse on your mother than being in an accident?"

—"*Yes, I fantasized passionately about being kidnapped, to make her recognize the absurdity of her attitude towards me, to force her to ask my forgiveness. I cried as much from sadness at being abandoned as from rage, on account of seeming weak . . . Our* [the children's] *demands were always ridiculous, ludicrous, in the eyes of our parents.*"

—"Both of them?"

—"*Yes, on that point, Mom and Dad were in agreement: in making fun of us. We weren't people.*"

To ex-sist, apart from parental control

Vera begins the second year of her treatment, and seems to be making decisive progress towards a certain liberation, enabling her to achieve more personal satisfaction. But in the period between her civil wedding ceremony and her church wedding (scheduled for just after Christmas), Vera suddenly tells me that she would like to reduce the number of her sessions from three to two a week.

—"*It seems to me that I can do it now, that I'm capable of it*", she declares at the end of a session, giving me the impression that she sees this as a sort of weaning.

In the following session, I decide to tell her that it doesn't seem advisable at this time to cut back on her sessions, that it would be better for her to maintain herself in the best possible conditions in order to further her analytic work, and that she can interrupt her treatment at a later time, if she wishes. Vera receives this opinion with obvious reserve; she will begin to manifest a certain hostility towards me—very discreet, but completely new. She says she is hurt by the fact that I don't seem to think her capable; it's as though I were claiming to know better than she does . . .

—"Like who?"

—"*Yes, of course, in that you're like my mother!*"

Vera's church wedding coincided with a ten-day interruption of the sessions occasioned by my own Christmas vacation. During the first session afterwards, Vera speaks of *"feeling down"* after the euphoria of the wedding; she felt very happy that day, as though she were *"fulfilled"*. Now, she observes, it's like having the *"baby blues"* (she uses the English term) after giving birth. She was worried about spending her honeymoon/vacation at the home of her in-laws; she would have preferred to stay alone with her husband a little while. Her parents-in-law have, she says, *"a tendency to infantilize us. In fact, with them, I irresponsibilize myself"*.

—She goes on: *"Before, when I lived at my parents' house, I used to tell myself that Mom could explode at any moment, or else collapse. She was capable of unleashing a tantrum at us, and I knew I couldn't rely on my brother or sister—or on my father, of course. I could only rely on myself. So I would try to prevent it by anticipating it: I would depress myself as if I had already been scolded."*

—"A kind of preventive self-scolding?"

—*"Yes, in order to stress myself, so that I'd be ready to act. I had the impression of being the only responsible person.*

"It's like with planning to have a baby. We would like to have one. But in that, I behave as if it depended on me alone! I mean, I'm haunted by the idea of not being capable of it. When I hear of some other woman not being able to have a child, I panic. If there are problems to be had, I am sure to have them; and they can only come from me. I need for everything to depend on me".

—"So, we easily pass back and forth between incapacity and omnipotence ..."

—*"I have the constant impression of not being mistress of my own body."*

—"There are things that do indeed escape you: like the functioning of your ovaries, your fallopian tubes ..."

—*" ... In fact, I have the impression of being inhabited by a foreign body; for example, when my period doesn't come at the right time. In order to exist, I need for everything to depend on me.*

" I think you are off to a bad start, when you want a baby, if you

> are saying that everything depends on you alone. It bodes ill for the future: maternal possessiveness, or else, depreciation . . . I am afraid I'll reject the baby.
>
> "When I was a teenager, I kept a journal; it was very violent and I quickly threw it away."

—"How's that?"

—"It was probably a rejection of myself, because I'd been trying to be sincere. It was very morbid; but it was a relief to produce it—and also to throw it away."

—"Like vomiting it?"

—"Yes, it's more intellectual, but it comes down to the same thing. Now I would like to go back to writing, because I can live more in the present."

Over the following month, Vera analyses her rivalry with her brother, her mother's favourite. After her brother's birth, when she was 4 years old, Vera is said to have stopped eating for several days.

> "Later, when he would hit my sister and me, our mother would always defend him. Rather recently, I realized that Mom only made something good to eat when HE was there!"

She then informs me that she has persuaded her husband to call me to get the name of an analyst for himself, in such a way that I find it impossible to decline her request. She says that I am the only person whose advice she can trust. I feel it impossible to maintain a neutral abstention here.

And a few weeks later, Vera will announce that since I'm not in favour of reducing the number of her sessions, she has decided to stop them. She has discovered a bulimia specialist who uses a group method within a context of weekend retreats. She considers that this would be enough for now to consolidate her therapeutic gains and not risk a relapse. She feels curious about communicating in this way with "others" (bulimics) and argues that this approach would be "incompatible" with the continuation of her analysis with me.

ORAL DRIVE FUNCTIONING AND SUBJECTION

—"Ah? Why is that?" (I sense this notion of incompatibility holds a clue.)

—*"It's a purely material problem: the cost of two treatments would be too much for our budget."*

—"Our?" I reply with emphasis, thinking that one person's therapy might overshadow another's, in a sort of sibling rivalry.

—*"Oh, yes"*, she answers, *"I haven't spoken any more with you about that: my husband did meet with the person you suggested. He's supposed to see her again, I don't know . . . No, for me it's something else: it seems to me it requires too much effort to come three evenings a week. Right now, I feel constrained; I'm not sure I'm doing it for myself. I am the 'good analysand' with you. It reminds me of Confession at church when I was a teenager—I was really zealous, I overdid it, I invented sins for myself! . . . In fact, I never did understand the sense of going to Confession."*

—"And coming here?"

—*"I don't know any more. It has helped me enormously to exist, but now it seems there's a kind of trap in it. One day, you pointed out to me that I never leave any silence in my sessions, that I begin speaking from the very second I lie down. It's because I always tell myself that's my role and that you are there for that. But because of this, I don't belong to myself. But don't they say that silence can be fruitful?*

"I feel obligated to speak to you about myself, it's what you demand of me."

I think Vera's fear of subjection is preventing her from progressing in the process of appropriation (subjectivation) of her own story.

—I say: "Maybe you're afraid that, if you are silent for an instant, you withdraw yourself from me?" And I am thinking of the way she answers "Yes" to most of my interventions, only to go on speaking without taking them into account.

—*"It would be like a refusal . . .* [a brief silence follows, for the first time!] *. . . At least, in my bulimic attacks, no one intervenes . . .*

[silence again] *Although . . . In fact, it is as if I had to eat. Like here: I have to eat . . . uh! . . . to speak."*

I have to call her attention to her slip of the tongue, which she seems to want to ignore. Then she goes on:

—*"Bulimia was, in a way, the only space for enjoyment that I had—a release of tension, after which I would trivialize everything else: other people, everything! . . . In analysis, I'm not free at all; I take you too much into account. I have no space for freedom; what the other person thinks is my constant preoccupation, but that doesn't mean that I'm really interested in the other person—it's just hard for me to displease him.*

"My bulimia started when I found out that my life was really play-acting: that I only wanted to please, that I was a coward—for example, being happy not defending myself, like a little saint! When I furiously wanted to punch people! My friendships always had an idyllic beginning, and then my need to exist would become incompatible and lead to a break-up."

—I say: "You may notice how that has recurred here: idyllic beginning, as you say, with spectacular results, and now you have to break it off in order to exist."

—*"My life is entirely like that: in pieces . . . There are people who remind me too much of Mom, who dispossess me of myself."*

—"So, it seems that you find your mother a little too much here?"

—*"Yes, as you don't speak much, her image imposes itself and keeps me from existing, demanding that I sacrifice myself. I'd like to know how people like me can get over it. I look for first-hand accounts of bulimia in books . . . but . . ."*

—"They leave you hungry . . ."

—"Yes", she laughs, *"it's an always unsatisfied hunger. That's the value of a group situation where you have to react, taking off your masks; that's why I'm tempted by this group of bulimics. The person I saw showed me a video where people are recounting their experiences. That interests me. But she presented herself as THE great specialist, the person who knows all about the issue! She advised me not to go on with the analysis, saying that I was too fragile . . . There! That's Mom's way of talking again.*

"You, on the other hand, don't seem to be against my wish to try out this group experience. In fact, I'm not honest regarding my analysis here: I have to admit that it has completely transformed me. I feel that I'm finally working on the real problems."

I have the impression then that she is undertaking a sort of identification with my non-possessiveness, based on her perception of my own acceptance of *passivation*.

A week later she will announce: *"My husband and I are going to have a baby! I'm mad with joy! It's too good to be true. It took my parents three years to make me. There was a miscarriage first. After that, they said that it was forced labour! . . ."*

She says now that she wants to continue her analysis during her pregnancy—to help her become a *"not too bad mother"*. She has also decided to go to the next weekend meeting of the group for bulimic patients. Afterwards, she will calmly tell me what she found interesting and profitable for her in these meetings.

At this point, I can realize that the trap of the transference (a transference of alienating subjection) had come close to shutting, in a way that would have proved fatal for the continuation of the treatment. I perceive in retrospect that what was at stake was mainly Vera's escape from the other's totalitarian (maternal) control—and her own which mirrored it—and that this had to be played out through my own acceptance of a phase of *passivation*.

She says: *"In my family life, there was never any advice, only orders; I had a lot of trouble realizing that it could be otherwise in my present relationships"*, at work also.

Vera has more surprises in store for me. First, in her second month of pregnancy, she announces that her fetus is dead. I feel concerned about the possible psychic effect of such a devastating event; but after her pained reaction to the initial shock, she will seem rather relieved to have been given some time to live her life before having to assume the role of mother. In addition, losing a first baby makes her like her mother—Vera herself having been born after a miscarriage—and the mother has reacted to Vera's miscarriage in a warm, supportive way.

But my biggest surprise comes when Vera speaks of the evolution of her relationship with her parents, especially with her mother. She is amazed to realize how the latter now accepts and even appreciates that Vera can stand up for her own opinions and tastes, starting with the wedding plans—rather as, in the end, I did not perceive myself disavowed by her experience of the weekend group sessions.

Conclusion

I would say, with reference to my commentary on "Instincts [drives] and Their Vicissitudes [destinies]", that Vera managed to establish a genuine, flexible interplay of turning around/reversal movements in her relationship with her mother (and with me). She now seems to be able to take pleasure in reversing position—from active to passive, from dominating to dominated, and vice versa.

In cases like this, where neurotic defences are associated with much more primary processes aimed at escaping from a substantial (feeding) relationship, we can experience a sort of transference of *subjection* where the patient blocks the psychoanalytic process—insofar as subjection thwarts *subjectivation*. Then the key for overcoming that kind of alienated transference seems to be on the analyst's part: he has to send signals of "displaying himself", as Freud says (1915c), getting something done by the patient to him/herself, in order to allow the patient to experience a reversal of the drive exchange.

At such a very regressive, primary level of transference, we probably reach what must have been in play at a very early stage of development, when the signification of maternal responses and initiatives in the drive exchanges will determine the possibilities of nascent *subjectivation*—that is, the child's ability to appropriate and recognize his/her own drive movements. Such a basic problematic certainly enters into play much before anything like a recognizable "object" can be acquired.

The progress made in this treatment was mainly due to the patient's capacity for representing to herself and verbalizing the problematic that was holding her captive. It must be said that the alienation she was suffering from did not go so far as to obliterate her fantasy activity.

A lack of fantasy is the major stumbling block for many other people who do not have Vera's aptitude for representation at the outset and thus have trouble engaging in a classic psychoanalytic treatment. Patients with behavioural, psychosomatic, or delusive symptomatologies will need to go through a preliminary therapeutic process to help them become the subject of a fantasy.

We will now treat, in chapter 3, the crucial question of the formation of fantasy as an essential step in the process of *subjectivation*.

Note

1. Three sessions of this case were discussed in a Franco–American meeting (CAPS) in Paris, 1998.

CHAPTER THREE

"A Child Is Being Beaten": the three stages of the subjectivation of fantasy

In Freud's 1919 study "A Child Is Being Beaten" (1919e), he clearly continues the development of his theorization of drive destinies (1915c). Proposing to shed light on the origin of perversions, Freud will raise, I think, the question of the ways in which *fantasy is subjectivated*; and he will depict this subjectivation as taking place through the positional *turning around* of drive destiny. More precisely, he will pinpoint the stage of *passivation*—the reversal of the drive's aim into a passive one—as essential to the subjective appropriation of personal enjoyment. Although the term *subject* does not appear as such in this text, Freud here attempts to describe the steps by which a drive representative (a sadomasochistic one in this case) may be subjectively appropriated in fantasy.

It is striking to note that this text is constructed according to the same scheme as "Instincts [drives] and Their Vicissitudes [destinies]" (1915c). In the first part (Chaps. 1 to 3), Freud attempts to describe the three successive positional configurations of the protagonists of the beating scenario, in such a way as to arrive at a generally applicable model. In a second part (Chap. 4), he examines this same process from the perspective of the libidinal economy, with the *demand for love* that can come into play there. Finally, a third part (Chaps. 5 and 6) develops his preoccupation with the origin of perversions. Here I shall focus only on the first part, the one that describes the succession of the subjective positions in question.

Freud first concentrates on showing the plurality of subjects that intervene as protagonists in the scenario he is examining. "As regards the early and simple phantasies", he says, "further information would have been welcome. *Who* was the child that was being beaten? *The one* who was himself producing the phantasy or *another*? Was it always *the same* child or as often as not *a different one*? *Who* was it that was beating the child? A grown-up person? And if so, *who*? Or did the child imagine that *he* himself was beating *another one*?" (p. 181). So we see various subject-equivalents appearing (which I have italicized); further on, Freud will employ the term *person* and, finally, the first-person pronoun, *I* [*Ich*].

Using material provided by four of his female patients—among them his own daughter Anna, as Georges and Sylvie Pragier have so helpfully called to our attention—Freud derives a description of a typical three-stage phenomenon.

1. He evokes a first phase in the representation of the beating, situated at "a very early period of childhood" (p. 184), which is characterized by the fact that "the child being beaten is never the one producing the phantasy, but is invariably another child, most often a brother or a sister if there is any."

At this phase, he considers that "the phantasy, then, is certainly not masochistic. It would be tempting to call it sadistic, but one cannot neglect the fact that the child producing the phantasy is never doing the beating *her*self." We should note that the child is referred to as "her" (emphasis mine).

The one doing the beating is an adult, who will turn out to be none other than the girl's father. This first stage of the scenario may therefore be formulated as follows: *the father is beating the child*. Thus three subjects take part in this action: one who is the *agent* of the beating (the father), one who *is getting himself beaten* (the other child), and, lastly, the one who is *representing* the scene to herself (the patient as child). These are the three possible ways of participating *as a subject* in a such a scenario.

Here, Freud feels the need to make a brief anticipatory allusion to the second part of this work, which will deal more with the imaginary content tied to the issue of love, with its conflicting significations. "I am betraying a great deal of what is to be brought forward later when instead of this I say: My father is beating the child *whom I hate*."

But Freud then returns to an essential question, that of knowing "whether the characteristics of a 'phantasy' can yet be ascribed to this first step towards the later beating-phantasy. It is perhaps rather a question of recollections of events which have been witnessed . . ." He thus wonders if this is not still a matter of *perceptive memories* that have not yet been organized into genuine fantasy. We see that Freud maintains a methodological doubt about whether this first representative stage of the scenario already constitutes a subjectivated fantasy in the psyche.[1] The fact of being a *subject of fantasy* is precisely what Freud refuses to consider as given, still less as automatic, at this first stage of the process—whence the indefinite mood of his title "A Child Is Being Beaten".

2. Important positional transformations must still be accomplished, he believes, in order to arrive at fantasy organization. He envisions a second phase, wherein "the person beating remains the same (that is, the father); but the child who is beaten has been changed into another one and is now invariably the child producing the phantasy."

This representation is now "accompanied by a high degree of pleasure, and has now acquired a significant content, with the origin of which we shall be concerned later" (p. 185). Freud will call this second stage of the scenario: *"I am being [will be] beaten by [my] father."* The appearance of the pronoun *I* [*ich*] will take into account the new subjective involvement—which of course recalls the famous Freudian formula: *Soll ich werden* . . .

According to Freud, the scenario has now taken on an indubitably *"masochistic"* character—at least this is the term he cannot avoid using to speak of seeking to satisfy the drive in a passive way. But this second phase, to which he attributes a key role in the process of subjectivation of fantasy, he qualifies at the same time as *virtual*, in the sense "that it has never had a real existence. It is never remembered, it has never succeeded in becoming conscious. It is a construction of analysis, but it is no less a necessity on that account" (p. 185). It is thus entirely in keeping with the perspective of "Instincts and Their Vicissitudes" that Freud sees the specific mode of subjective appropriation in the conjunction of *turning around upon one's own body* and *reversal into the opposite* (*passive satisfaction*) of the drive aim.

3. The third phase, on the other hand, is directly familiar to us, Freud says, for it is explicit in the patient's speech in analysis, in the material provided by the sessions. Its positional configuration (topic) resembles that of the first stage, except that the person beating is never the father, but either is left undetermined or turns into a substitute, such as a teacher. "The figure of the child who is producing the beating phantasy no longer itself appears in it. In reply to pressing inquiries, the patients only declare: 'I am probably looking on.' Instead of the one child that is being beaten, there are now a number of children present as a rule" (p. 186). In Freud's female patients' fantasies, these are boys, and he insists on an essential difference between this third phase and the first: "the phantasy now has strong and unambiguous sexual excitement attached to it, and so provides a means for masturbatory satisfaction."

This is precisely the important question for Freud: "By what path has the phantasy of strange and unknown boys being beaten (a phantasy which has by this time become sadistic) found its way into the permanent possession of the little girls' libidinal trends?" In other words, I would say, sadism has now taken on all its charge of subjective enjoyment. The capacity for making oneself the subject of sadistic attitudes in fantasy necessitates a preliminary stage (the second phase) of "masochistic" subjectivation. Freud suggests then that subjectivated sadism would result from a masochistic position (*passivation*) experienced in fantasy, and secondarily turned around upon others.

Through this exemplary beating fantasy in girls, with its levels of libidinal appropriation, we see how erroneous it would be to confuse the process of subjectivation with that of becoming conscious. In the third phase, the fantasy attains its full libidinal (and preconscious) charge, at the same time acquiring a more pronounced *defensive* dimension—with repression by the ego necessitating, Freud says, a whole work of psychoanalysis. So not only should the subject of fantasy not be assimilated to the instance of consciousness, but our reading of Freud encourages us not to confuse the reinforcement of this drive subject (animating and misunderstood) with the integrating and defensive function of the ego.

The implication of drive subject in fantasy

Fantasy could be defined as the putting into psychic representation of a *relationship* in which the subject is implicated. Michèle Perron-Borelli (1997) has even argued that this relationship is necessarily an *action*—which is in line with my views concerning the basic role of drive transaction in any subjectivating process. Nevertheless, it should be recalled that not every *image* is a fantasy: a mere hallucination, for example, is not enough to constitute a fantasmatic relationship wherein one is implicated as subject. On this point, Freud's meticulous reconstruction of the possible origin in reality of the Wolf Man's fantasy is only in apparent disagreement with his views in "Instincts and Their Vicissitudes", which he was writing at about the same time. For what basically fuels Freud's research into the Wolf Man's case is precisely the reconstitution of *perceptive traces that have failed to be organized as fantasy*—and this failure may very well have been the cause of the patient's difficulties in performing his treatment(s).

I would express one reservation regarding Perron-Borelli's argument insofar as she goes on to say that the construction of fantasy coincides with *subjectivation* itself. Indeed, it seems to me that the *putting into figurative representation* (of the relationship between oneself and any object) does not constitute the whole of the process of subjectivation, even if, of course, it does attest to the final constitution of psychic reality. I have already insisted on the fact that subjectivation is born in the drive exchanges with the parental other, involving turnings-around/reversals that we have every reason to think are established and inscribed before the person proper is able to constitute a figurative representation of itself. Regarding this, I would add that cenesthesic representations (the sensations of one's body in space) probably precede any visual holistic figuration of oneself, which recently led various authors, such as Claude Le Guen (2001), to insist on the role of "motor representations" in the early psychic development.

Here again we run up against a notorious problem: the use of the term *object* in psychoanalysis (I shall come back to this in chapter 8, when I discuss sublimation). There is, in fact, an irreducible gap between the obscure (and necessarily lost) object of the drive (Freud's *das Ding*—the thing) and the object-as-other, which has to re-present the object of the drive if it is to be represented as a protagonist in the fantasy, where it will appear in a relationship with the subject (as we can see in most dreams).

Lacan tried to render this by means of a formula for fantasy, $ \diamond a$, whose paradoxical character we notice, since not one of its three terms—the lozenge symbolizing the relationship (or interaction), the subject $, the little *a* object—has *spatial–corporal* figuration in itself! So that neither the subject nor the object (*a*) can be represented except indirectly, through imaginary substitutes (the ego, the other, natural objects, etc.).

According to the logic of what we have proposed here, we have every reason to think that proper subjectivation begins much before any acquisition of a figurative image of oneself (or any organized ego). The construction of fantasy could then accomplish a kind of *translation* into figurative terms (as well cenesthesic or acoustic ones) of what may have been experienced in the founding drive interactions. But such a translation can be a *transforming one*, capable even of reversing what was experienced at the origin.

In extreme pathological organizations (psychoses), certain fantasies even appear to be desperate attempts at subjectivating a founding relationship that is impossible to experience. This is especially the case of the self-engenderment fantasies that some schizophrenics construct to compensate for the symbolic deficit that inhabits them. Another famous example is given in the autobiographical essay of President Schreber (Freud, 1911c [1910]) where we see how fantasy activity can strive to take over from the delusive experience, in order to make *mentally treatable* what seems to have been something real but impossible to assimilate:

the dehumanizing experience ("soul murder") he suffered at the hands of his torturer–orthopaedist father.

I have already alluded to Freud's stubborn efforts to find some perceptive traces in his patient, the Wolf Man—whose distress was precisely the result of a certain deficiency in his implication as a subject in a fantasized *primal scene*. The famous "primal scene phantasy" that Freud will emphasize thereafter exemplifies the way in which each individual subject must, on his own behalf, represent for himself the very relationship from which his own engenderment as a subject is conceivable.

The primary narcissistic fantasy

The view of construction of fantasy I am promoting here could appear to contradict the notion of *primary narcissistic fantasy*, which Freud posited when he introduced the concept of narcissism (1914c). Freud used this notion to pursue another idea he seems to have cherished, that of an initial stage of auto-eroticism in human development. He describes the primary narcissistic fantasy as feeling oneself to be almighty, in a state of completeness and harmony with the world (I think a good literary example would be the state of elation described by Lamartine in his poem "The Lake").

I think it interesting to examine here the extent to which such a narcissistic fantasy can stand in opposition to the considerations about fantasy construction developed above. I would like to make some observations about this.

First, we have no reason to think that such a primary narcissistic fantasy would escape from the common rule for any fantasy organized in the psychic apparatus: that it must be constituted *afterwards*, out of effective drive interactions experienced between the baby and its mother (we now believe that some of these might begin *in utero*!).

This said, the primary narcissistic fantasy presents one peculiar characteristic: it mixes up the protagonists of the first drive experiences. For here the child attributes to itself the power that it has perceived in its parent, especially at the moment of *passivation* of drive satisfaction (getting oneself looked at, getting oneself taken in hand).

It appears however that the primary narcissistic fantasy does respect a subject/object arrangement, as long as the object is considered to be none other than the ego itself—but in this case, it is a *nascent ego,* which as such includes the perceived power of the parental protagonist.

We could even go so far as to observe that it is within the range of fantasies called "narcissistic" that a certain gap between subject and ego may best be manifested, the ego simply taking the place of the object within the fantasy relationship.

The necessary dis-completing *of the parental other*

Let us return now to the fact that the drive subject is constructed in interaction with the drive response coming from the parental other. This response actually constitutes a form of involvement of this other (even before it is perceived as an other) and presupposes, shall we say, a certain *avowal* (the opposite of a *disavowal*) on the part of the latter. In the best of cases, indeed, the parent's response shows how well he/she can stand to be desiring—that is, how well he/she can tolerate the feeling of lacking something. I have elsewhere (Penot, 1989) evoked this characteristic of the nascent subject: that it necessarily puts into play the *"dis-completeness" of the mother*—she who is first imagined by the very small child as *having everything,* a phallic mother (like the famous Artemis of the Ephesians). In the next chapter, we will come back to the fundamental fact that the nascent subject must tolerate the perception of a *dis-completeness* inflicted on the parent by the child's *ex-sistence* (along with the unbinding that this implies). But such an aptitude in the child will largely depend on the parental partner's ability to experience this *subtraction* in a positive way, without it becoming a major narcissistic trauma leading to a withdrawal of his/her love.

We have seen that this is just what Vera (chapter 2) had believed impossible to obtain from her mother. In the next chapter, the therapeutic history of a difficult adolescent girl, who had to be treated in an institutional setting, can illustrate the key function of such a parental capacity in enabling the patient to overcome a generational impasse.

Note

1. Here is material for re-investigating the so-called originary fantasies. Indeed, the latter expression seems to promote the idea of a natural and even, in a way, "endogenous" production of fantasy. The debate around this issue recalls that about "typical dreams".

CHAPTER FOUR

The misfortunes of Sophie, or the *bad subject* to come

Nowadays we frequently have to deal with so-called borderline cases with *pathological behaviours* that give the impression of a drama being replayed indefinitely. With many adolescents in particular, we suspect the presence of some psychic determinism that the youngster in question may be unable to *subjectivate* into a personal discourse, and which therefore takes the form of acts. The psychoanalyst finds him/herself in the paradoxical position of *not being able to rely on the youngster's own speech* to provide the keys to understanding the alienation from which he or she is so obviously suffering.

Here the ordinary spoken encounter between patient and analyst proves unsuited at the outset as an aid to recovery. This is the case with those common problems that are lumped under the heading of *academic phobia*, and which usually lead the teenager to serve up a vaguely rationalizing or fabricating discourse, without given any effective clue as to what is actually hampering him as a subject.

It is precisely this deficiency in the verbal exchange that makes it advisable to approach such youngsters within an institutional setting. But what kind of setting is best suited to fostering the advent of true speech, working towards the emergence of the *"bad subject"* (Lacan, 1959)[1] within them, giving them the means to *subjectivate* their behaviours and make them capable of rendering an account of them? Experience with so-called behavioural pathologies teaches the psychoanalyst the usefulness of buttressing his/her practice with a framework set up to fulfil two essential conditions:

The analyst must first ensure that the young patient's distress is received in a genuine *space for living*—that is, a place where effective drive exchanges are possible, which is at the same time a *"transitional"* space (Winnicott) where the youngster can find a response to his/her attempts at understanding his/her drives. It is not a space where technical interventions are distributed in the form of various individual or group sessions, though these are indeed frequent; it is, rather, a milieu whose goal is to enable, through experiences we live through together, the *birth of a mutual discourse*.

A second condition follows as a corollary to the first: the youngster's treatment must be connected *with concurrent work with and by his/her original milieu—that is, his or her family*. In this, it is good that the work of exchange and putting into words take place regularly between the family and the therapists most directly involved on a daily basis in exchanges with the patient. In our hospital, these therapists (psychologists or educators) are called the patient's *referents,* and usually work in male–female pairs.

This does, in fact, prove to be the condition most favourable to turning shared experience into speech, through its very repetition in the present. Indeed, it is through what may be formulated concerning what we are experiencing together in the present that we can better revisit the more or less veiled traumatic experiences in the family's history—according to the model of the *transference* in the treatment. In so doing we must take seriously the *acted repetition* insofar as it manifests an agent of the drive that lacks subjectivation, due to a signifying relation that has been defective since the start.

The case of "Sophie"

The history of Sophie's treatment can illustrate how the emergence of a subject of discourse requires that (acted) drive impulsion receives a sufficiently meaningful response from the partner—especially where its symbolization has been defective.

This very personable adolescent was referred to us at our day hospital[2] at the age of 13 on account of serious conduct disorders that began to appear when she was in preschool—marked by a refusal of the school setting and many very disturbing passages to the act. She was spoken of as being in a serious childhood *psychotic* state, with no intellectual deficiency. Striving to reconstruct the very eventful history of the preceding years, I learned that after having run away from home several times and endangered herself in various ways, Sophie was, at the age of 10, sent to a boarding school in the southwest of France. Her parents had decided to send her there after she had taken a rather startling initiative: she is said to have gone around the neighbourhood *selling*, for a few francs a piece, all the objects her parents had received as wedding presents! This was too much for the family, so Sophie was sent to boarding school, which had a rather positive effect on her during the first year, when she more or less kept up with the fifth grade. But the passage into sixth grade—that is, out of elementary school—the following year, into a nearby middle school, brought on new turbulence. At one point Sophie even climbed up onto the roof of the school and threatened to jump. She was then sent home to her parents—but not before having beaten up an educator.

When I first meet Sophie a year later, her parents are completely worn out, overwhelmed by an unceasing onslaught of events. There is also the fact that Sophie cannot fall asleep by herself. Family members have to take turns keeping her company in bed—her mother, of course, when she is at home (as a nurse, she has to work some nights), or her father, or her little brother, plus the cat. Sophie does seem to experience visual hallucinatory phenomena at night, though it is hard to get her be more specific about this: her discourse immediately turns into an overflowing imaginary gush, extremely fluctuating and uninformative.

However, she is said to have spoken recently to the colleague who referred her to us (and is still treating her in a clinic) about the image of "a rather old man" who would command her to do mean or sexual things. We will meet with this again later.

Sophie's parents come from the same village in central Italy—a fact that conflicts with the sharply contrasted aspect of the couple: the mother is blond and willowy, with a slightly mysterious reserve, while the father is swarthy and hirsute. During the interviews, she dominates the exchange, reducing the father to a silent, thwarted presence, whom she does not consult when making decisions. Both parents settled in Paris after the Second World War.

We advise a monthly meeting, which for three years will bring together Sophie, her parents, the psychiatrist (myself), and the pair of caregivers (a female psychologist and a male educator) who are Sophie's referents in the day hospital. The father will be physically present, but he seems to have no opinion; it will take us nearly two years to establish a collaboration with him. It seems accepted in the family that Sophie's upbringing is entirely up to her mother.

The latter manifests a kind of complicity in her daughter's shenanigans, giving the impression of a *narcissistic seduction*. She disowns her husband's attempts to intervene, which she judges to be "brutal". As for Sophie, she openly scorns her father. When she insults him during the session, he does not react at all, which obliges me to intervene sometimes. In addition, she actively contributes to what seems to be jealousy on the father's part.

The mother is rather attractive, in fact, but in the manner of the "Indifferent Beauty", always acting surprised to hear people talk about how attractive she is to men, as if she couldn't understand. . . . At home, Sophie carefully intercepts phone calls meant for her mother, apparently from male co-workers (nurses). Sophie also claims that her father is sexually brutal with her mother, and that the children are all aware of this.

But the impression we are left with is not that the parents are mismatched—as is often the case in our work with families—but, rather, that their relationship is more like some kind of confusing, incestuous cousinship.

As for Sophie herself, she will be rather *sociable* in the day hospital, though in an impetuous, manipulative way—both with the adolescents she sets her sights on and with the adults, caregivers, and teachers. The latter are disconcerted by the contrast between

Sophie's obvious intelligence and the impossibility of pursuing any sort of work with her, whether spoken or written.

In one way or another, she is always involved in delinquent acts committed in the day hospital—rackets, thefts, provocations intended to endanger some other person. Sophie seems to be affected by what happens to her, and she defends herself with a mixture of vehemence and bad faith. She is highly interested in sexual matters but never gets physically involved, preferring to attach herself parasitically to other people's experiences.

It is mainly while discussing vacation plans with Sophie and her parents that we will gain a better understanding of some characteristics of the parents' respective families. The status of men turns out to be paradoxical: while ostensibly dominant (the mother says that women are relegated to the kitchen at mealtime, while the men lounge around the dining-room table), the men appear to be submitted to the women's discourse whenever there is a decision to make, especially concerning the children.

The mother says that she is the only one of her parents' children who completed high school (she went on to get a nursing degree). During her youth at home, she had to assume the chore often delegated to the children of immigrants: that of filling out government forms and even of keeping the accounts. She describes two of her sisters as illiterate and possibly retarded (one of them is epileptic).

Little by little, we will manage to get this somewhat *distant* woman better involved and, at the same time, arrive at more effective cooperation between the two parents. During the second year at the day hospital, the tension at home between Sophie and her father will become more explicit, with the latter starting to declare that he is displeased and opposed to certain excesses. He threatens to put his daughter out if she does not respect certain hours. In our interviews, he looks to the caregivers for support, while the mother seems to distance herself behind her nursing credentials. This distancing is all the more disconcerting in that Sophie is out of control at the moment, stealing her mother's credit card, for example, and taking many of her mother's objects, clothes and shoes, into her room, where she stashes them under her bed. Here the family has reached the critical threshold of a relationship system that Paul-Claude Racamier (1995) designated as *"incestuel"* (not exactly incestuous), where there is a permanent porosity and violation of each other's private space, without sexual acts.

Sophie sleep problems have disappeared, however. From now on she can come alone on the commuter train and go out with her friends without getting into much mischief. She has become a rather beautiful, well-groomed girl, though her skinniness worries some of the caregivers. She speaks of becoming a cosmetician. Since she has practically stopped attending the high-school courses planned for her in the day hospital, we are starting to wonder, at the end of her second year, if it wouldn't be better to see her in *post-treatment* the following year, with her having some training programmes outside.

In the meantime, her Easter vacation in Italy will be a revelation. Having travelled alone with her paternal grandfather (the grandmother refused to go along) to the village that her whole family came from, Sophie will be practically sequestered by her grandfather, who claims it is because of family quarrels.

Upon her return, she gives us a colourful account of this, also reporting salacious remarks her grandfather is supposed to have made about Sophie's mother, whom the grandfather said he'd like to *screw* the next time he met her. . . .

The parental acknowledgement

Upon hearing this account during the next family meeting after Sophie's return, her father will confirm, with some embarrassment, that his father is in fact "perfectly capable of acting that way with family". This validation of what his daughter had said, coming after some other, less important acknowledgements, will help to confer upon her an increasing ability to posit herself as the *subject* of speech and initiatives.

But a more surprising phenomenon will occur. The father declares suddenly, with an embarrassed laugh, that *he has not the slightest memory of his own childhood, or even of his adolescence*. His earliest memory is from when he was 17 years old—and then we realize together that this is the age at which he began his relationship with Sophie's mother.

During the following months, and up until the summer vacation, it will become clear that Sophie's speech is acquiring a more pertinent quality—although it can easily be impertinent! Her speech carries more weight, and she intervenes in a positive way when there are disputes among youngsters at the hospital. With the help of an educational psychologist at the hospital, she begins to work on a genealogy of her family and also starts individual work in mathematics.

When the hospital reopens in September, we are surprised to learn that in July Sophie was able to do a month-long summer internship in the garage where her father works. The father's boss declared that he was pleased with her; there were no incidents. We are especially struck by the remarkable transformation in the relationship between father and daughter: this man now seems able to sustain his daughter in her positive actions, and she has ceased to denigrate and humiliate him. We cannot help but observe how the father's *confession*, in the presence of his wife and daughter, brought about a change in the imaginary relation in the latter. Let us say that *true speech*—speech filled with affect—on the part of this man, in the form of self-acknowledgement concerning his traumatic childhood, seemed to have inspired consideration in his daughter and to have made it possible for identification to pass between them.

We will experience a third year with Sophie in the day hospital, bringing with it new internships (she will work whole days for several months in a retirement home, and then in a clinic), as well as the beginning of secretarial training. But the benefits will be most noticeable in the quality of Sophie's personal way of expressing herself and in her ability to get involved in friendships with other young people.

The brief narrative of this institutional treatment can, starting with a pathology that is essentially behavioural and violent and an *empty speech* (Lacan) endlessly going astray in a frantic search for *release*, illustrate how present-day experience that was commented upon helped to solidify a discourse that gives an account of the neo-history lived together. The regular meetings allowed for the construction of a shared *mythic* discourse, with a putting into images and into words ensuring a lasting binding of traumatic impressions acted out in the family. Such work of signifying connection, gradually giving an account of the drive interaction in play, reinforced in Sophie a *subject function* in her speech and her acts.

This kind of therapeutic case history certainly appears far removed from the conditions of the classic analytic treatment. But it is rather representative of a type of pathology whose frequency now seems to be invading our societal space. Therapeutic work of the kind described here has the advantage of reminding the psychoanalyst how slavish, *"de-subjectivated"* activity can come to engender more subject function once it has managed to obtain a response in the form of an acknowledgement by the parental other—a response that must be obtained as long as *fantasy* has not been able to be sufficiently built in the intrapsychic world.

Regarding the case we have been discussing here, it is not surprising that the father's decisive acknowledgement, received by the daughter as being charged with genuine affect, was the acknowledgement of a *lack—of something he'd suffered*. But Sophie was lucky enough to benefit from a remarkable effort at participation on her parents' part. They were able to overcome their own narcissistic defences, in the form of a *disavowal* on the part of each one of his or her traumatic history, in order to join us in a process of verbalization that directly involved them.

Note

1. Lacan qualifies the subject that constitutes the aim of psychoanalysis as being the "bad subject" of desire—more or less repressed, or even *"foreclosed"*—which he opposes to the "good subject of philosophical knowledge": "Freud makes the good subject of philosophical knowledge definitively disappear, the subject who found in the object a sure status, before the bad subject of desire and its impostures" (Lacan, 2006, p. 599).

2. This is the Cerep-Montsouris day hospital for adolescents, in the 14th arrondissement of Paris.

CHAPTER FIVE

Adolescence of the Freudian subject

What this book has to say about the emergence of the subject function as related to drive is fed by clinical work with adolescents in particular. Indeed, adolescence is inaugurated precisely by what I propose to call a *change in the drive system*—that is, the phenomenon of the *pubertaire* (Gutton, 1991), which consecrates the manifest rupture with childhood.

In practice, it is by means of this *pubertaire* step (which is first a physiological one) that the entry into adolescence is ordinarily determined; however, at the other extreme, at the exit from adolescence, it will be mainly social criteria that will allow us to determine whether a young person has attained adult status. It is interesting to note that each term of this double boundary that delineates adolescence has the characteristic of being situated outside the area proper to psychology! But the psychoanalyst will be able to find in this observation evidence confirming the swaying between, on the one hand, the putting into play of drive renewal in its *real* dimension and, on the other hand, the emergence from the subject of new *symbolic exchanges*.

My practice, which has been partly dedicated to adolescents in great subjective distress, has led me to see in adolescent crisis the model for every transforming existential passage. By the same token, I have gradually come to notice how in most adult psychoanalytic treatments the transference begins to take hold precisely at the point where the adolescent process failed, where its development was arrested.[1] The generations of psychoanalysts who have gone before us undoubtedly took too long to recognize (in spite of Anna Freud) that, after all, the *infantile neurosis* of our adult patients in analysis only lets itself be known through the transforming rearrangement imposed upon it by the adolescent process. . . .

At the manifest level of every case, the adolescent crisis itself will first of all take the form of an overturning of "imaginary" landmarks. First, the register of *narcissistic supports* will be placed in difficulty on account of the shake-up produced by the change of the drive system at puberty. In the adolescent who is suffering, the *image of his or her own body* will be shaken up first; but this crisis situation will also entail a destabilization of the *ideal figures* who have hitherto acted as imaginary referents for the child. So the adolescent will have to construct other ones.

Jean-Jacques Rassial has said (1990) that "adolescence is an age where the imaginary matters" (but is there any age where the representation of the body doesn't matter? . . .). Regarding this, the clinical treatment of the Winnicottian *breakdown*, as it has been continued by Moses and Eglé Laufer (1984), provides an extreme illustration of the possible collapse of the narcissistic representation of oneself. Nevertheless, even in its most commonplace forms, adolescent crisis will shake up the narcissism at two levels.

First, there is the forced transformation of the corporal representation of oneself—as if the ego had to change its skin (one thinks of the *moi-peau*, or "ego-skin", coined by Didier Anzieu (1989), and, more concretely, of the skin eruptions so characteristic of adolescence). It is as if the childhood ego no longer has the stuff to contain the new drive motions that come to reactivate elements of infantile neurosis by bursting its too narrow frame.

But this necessary moulting of the ego will at the same time be accompanied by a crisis in the intrapsychic figures of reference—the *parental imagos,* as they are called. I chose to call one of my clinical presentations "When There Is Something Rotten in the Father", in order to better show, through the case of "Martin"

(Penot, 1989), how, in most adolescents in crisis, it is not so much the paternal psychic representative as symbolic referent that is called into question but, rather, its imaginary substance: the son is seized with doubt as to the *value* he can attribute to the father figure he has at his disposal.

Hamlet—still adolescent at 30—doubtless remains one of the great examples of this. He also serves to remind us that an adolescent, however afflicted, is still someone who can really hurt you—as Polonius perhaps had the time to realize (and Laius, too?). Though the analyst must, of course, evaluate the alienating potential of this crisis-ridden referential imaginary world, this narcissistic container (both egoical and superegoical) perceived as defective and "rotten", he or she must also evaluate its worth as an *imaginary support*. The question is indeed unavoidable: what will build up a youngster's ability to sustain him/herself as the subject of his/her own desires?

The emergence of the subject of a personal speech, and the conditions for this emergence, constitute the crucial issue of the adolescent passage (Cahn, 1991a), an issue corroborated *a contrario* by the peculiar frequency of psychotic breakdown at this age.

This follows because access to adulthood, at the same time as the effective sexual differentiation of one's own body, will provoke the decisive moment when one must *sustain oneself as a subject*—in the sense described above, that of an agent of drive activity. The adolescent is faced with the fact of being propelled towards physical similarity with his parent (when he doesn't become even taller than his father) and the pressure that he feels intimately, in his body and in his sex organs, is even more upsetting in that he also knows he is now endowed with a very real capacity for engendering a child.[2] The status of child has become subjectively untenable for him.

Sexual differentiation requires the adolescent to experience something like an *imaginary incompleteness*, in rupture with the more fluid ways of reference and subjection that prevailed during childhood. Sexual differentiation, becoming more effective, implies a certain *renunciation of the sex organ we don't have*; and since as far as we know, there is no subject but the human one—that is, a sexually differentiated one—the differentiation that occurs at puberty will trigger that exemplary ordeal by which the subject of such incompleteness will find him/herself unable to *ex-sist*.

It is probably inevitable that such a "new subject", as Freud calls it in "Instincts and Their Vicissitudes", will sorely test the formal supports that have until then served as containers during childhood (new skins for new wine, as the Scriptures say). Hence the necessity to construct others, in order to provide the adolescent subject with the imaginary stuff necessary for sustaining itself as a *psychic reality*.

In many adolescents in crisis, it is common to observe a characteristic wavering between active provocation and passive conformity; the alternating exacerbation of conducts marked by gregarious conformity and patently odd retreats into solitude, or between accentuation of sexual differentiation and recourse to *unisex* looks. This is the time of maximum work on the relationship, contradictory and necessary, between the processes of imaginary identification that constitute the ego (continued in the *ideal ego's* models of conformity) and the emergence of the subject of one's own desire through drive activity in search of means (these will come from that key psychic operator, the *ideal of the ego*).

Later (chapter 8) we will see how this last instance should be rooted in the child's first impressions of the effective operators of parental power—the *real father*, but also the mother's father—and not in the imaginary narcissistic projections that will form the figures of the *ideal ego*.[3]

As for the possible substance of the subject, it is interesting to recall how in the 1930s the learned authors Jacques Damourette and Edouard Pichon (uncle of Jacques Lacan and one of the founders of the Paris Psychoanalytical Society) tried to explain in their famous French Grammar the conceivable difference between the "maintained person" (I, you, he) and the "fleshed-out person" (me, you [as object], him)—a way of rendering an account of the respective attributes of the subject of the grammatical utterance (called the *shifter* by linguists) and the linguistic representatives of the spatio–corporal person (Damourette & Pichon, 1946).

It may also be useful to recall that, from a historical perspective, adolescent crisis was for a long time the privilege of the sons of wealthy families, while the majority of less privileged youngsters in the Paris region expressed themselves until quite recently in the well-known *"j'sommes"*, *"j'avons"* manner—contractions that ungrammatically slur the first-person singular noun into the first-person plural verb in a way that attests to the way these youths were kept at a stage before there was any question of taking on a singular subjective existence—the engulfing of their person in a collective *ego,* which spared them having to cross the critical threshold of adolescence....

We should also note the observable historical concurrence between the birth of psychoanalysis and the spread of the phenomenon of adolescence throughout society, at the threshold of our neo- or post-industrial era. Such a coincidence seems to me to suggest that the clinical forms of adolescent suffering have a particular calling: to pave the way towards a psychoanalytic theory of the subject.

However, judging from some colleagues' insistence on systematizing an opposition—dynamic, economic, and even structural—between adolescence and adulthood, one might suspect that their approach is based on the received (and rather sad) idea that adulthood ought to be a kind of neo-latency period.... Fortunately, this does not correspond to the professional experience of the psychoanalyst (nor, one would hope, to his or her personal life!), whether it concerns some patient in the throes of romantic heartache at 50, or another suddenly forced into early retirement, or a parent living every day through the shock of being intimately called into question by a teenaged son or daughter.[4]

So I would say that my interest in adolescents has, rather, been fed by the reverse perspective, that of considering adolescence in light of its *exemplary* quality. The critical and decisive moment of the passage to adulthood seems interesting to me above all because it most sharply illustrates the *condition of the human subject*—more precisely, the process by which a particular subject manages to emerge and sustain itself through the narcissistic upheavals that characterize this passage of life.

The provocation of crisis in the ideal imaginary references that generally characterize adolescence will highlight the need for the subject function to exercise itself in a repeated and effective play of drive activity—which is also corroborated by the teachings of *sublimation* (see chapter 8). Thus, when dealing psychotherapeutically with grave disorders of adolescence, it will be necessary for the therapist to adopt a kind of involvement that is not limited to the symbolic role of the *blue helmet*,[5] so to speak—the supposedly neutral observer of adolescent violence. . . .

These considerations lead me to reformulate my proposition as follows: if the approach to adolescent psychopathology seems potentially instructive for the psychoanalyst, it is not so much because of what it has that is specific and particular, but, rather, because of the *exemplariness* of what this clinical work unfurls before our eyes as the possible modalities for bringing forth the subject of one's own desire, by causing crisis in a framework of formal conformity, belonging to the ego and the superego.

The very particular frequency, at this time of life, of the manifest appearance of psychotic symptoms, especially the outbreak of *delusion*, proves this by default. In cases of psychosis, the differentiation of puberty and the narcissistic incompleteness that results from it tends to break down a blanket of narcissism and push the youngster into the breach thus produced in the imaginary unity and conformity that used to protect him. This is undoubtedly the *flaw* Freud talks about in "Neurosis and Psychosis" (1924b [1923]): that catastrophic hole opening up in the subject's relationship with his external reality, which will be plugged up by the eruption of delusion.

The rupture in the narcissistic support is such that it will necessitate the establishment of the delusion's neo-reality, defined by Freud as "a patch over the place where originally a rent had appeared in the ego's relation to the external world" (Freud, 1924b [1923], p. 151). The primary function of this delusive *patching* would thus be to serve as an expedient, a stop-gap, a plug, to which we would be wrong to attribute a value of meaning like that of the subjectivated productions of fantasy.

Through a case like that of young Paul (Penot, 1991), I have tried to illustrate how the delusive patch, applied so as to cover up a rip in the psychotic's relationship with what is, for him, reality (and conformity), is not in fact composed just of anything, but of something that has "already happened", as Freud says, in the individual's history or that of his family, of an *anachronistic* element whose failure to fit into the subject's psychic reality may be a result of the traumatic character it holds (for the family)—which is why it returns, *ghost-like* (Penot, 1996) in the form of delusion and hallucination.

If the analyst is prepared to get out of the couch–chair (or chair–chair) relation and listen to his delusive patients with their family entourage, he cannot help but see that the defect of binding, the flaw that maims their psychic reality, is not only observable in the patients themselves: something of it may also be appear in the psychic economy of the milieu of origin.

Ought we then consider the difficulty of thinking presented by the family milieu as a consequence of (a reaction to) the intrapsychic disturbance of the patient him/herself? It seems rather that the deficiency of symbolization afflicting the patient is rooted in a specific thought disorder within his/her original milieu: difficulty mentalizing something traumatic whose effect would grow more radical with each passing generation. This "impossible-to-think" may be apprehended through enigmatic parental messages, which seem meant to cover up some narcissistic damage, often related to unachieved mourning. The frequent recurrence of this kind of experience in family therapies leads me to think that *something can be traumatic for the child only if it has been traumatic for the parent*—that is, if it has overwhelmed the parent's own capacity for thought.

Some psychotic breakdowns in adolescence display all the characteristics of a traumatic state: the rejection of reality that dominates the clinical picture is clearly related to a defence against pain, commensurate with the overload of the capacity for symbolic connection caused by the impact of certain events. The avoidance of psychic pain dictates an extensive rejection of external reality, as well as of the interlocutor that we are trying to be (rejection that recalls Freud's reference to *paraphrenics*: 1914c, p. 74).

A tragic familial destiny

Our work in family therapy with adolescents presenting severe problems of mentalization will regularly lead us to note that the areas in which these youths display thought-blockage correspond to sectors where other family members, primarily the parents, seem themselves to be ill at ease. In the parents this typically takes on the appearance of a defensive blockage concerning *a mourning* that they had had to carry out, or a wound to their existence: the roads towards verbalization then seem impassable.

We observe that it is the very capacity for elaborating a *family myth* that is then compromised. Whatever the history of a family marked by major narcissistic suffering, protected as well as it can be by narcissistic defences (disavowal-splitting, for the most part), our therapeutic action should attempt to foster *more mythmaking* about elements of origins, basic material that is indispensable in building the narcissism of the most recent generation—more thinking by the family about itself, providing the conditions necessary for symbolic orientation and removing the prohibition that hinders the youngster's own appropriation of the fantasized heritage that belongs to him/her. Here one might say, slightly paraphrasing Jacques Lacan, that the family's mythic discourse tends to constitute for the younger generation a sort of *"ready-to-fantasize"*.

This was exemplified by the case of a girl of West African origin whom I will call Celeste. She was referred to me at the age of 16 by her local medical-psychological centre, where she had been known to the team for a year, since she used to bring her little brother Desiré there to be treated for childhood psychosis. It was then that she began to tell the staff about her own intense anxiety and insomnia. At that time Celeste was struggling through a business-oriented fourth form at a nearby middle school, where her feeling of being persecuted had caused her to adopt an attitude of constant subjective withdrawal. The staff at the centre then perceived that Celeste was steeped in uncanny experience: she was constantly gripped by a fear that something would happen to her, some fatal accident. The intensification of this fear brought about an "autistic" withdrawal, a disinvestment so great that the school would not accept her back. This is why she had applied to our day hospital for adolescents.

I first see Celeste with her mother, who seems very reticent, giving me to understand that she herself has already suffered much. The few elements of her history that she is willing to share are, in fact, very disturbing. She was very young when she became pregnant with Celeste, by a fellow African studying in Paris, who disappeared as soon as he learned of the pregnancy. But this man's brother, a devout Christian, endeavoured to persuade her that it would be a sin to have an abortion, and he offered to recognize the child in his brother's stead and give her his name. Because of this, Celeste bears the last name of a father she never knew.

The young mother did all she could to care for the child herself, against the advice of social services that she put the child up for adoption. One year later she married another compatriot, a journalist. This man was always affectionate towards Celeste, treating her as if she were his own daughter—and she called him *Daddy*. No one saw the point of giving Celeste any explanation as to why her surname differed from that of her "father"—and the mother is even now confused about this.

This mother's second union produced two children, Crystelle and Desiré. The latter was not yet 1 year old when his father died while visiting their native country. The father, barely 30 years old, was the victim of a neurological disease that the mother seems at pains to explain. This event still seems to be a disturbing mystery for the mother, who sees it as the latest in a series of tragic deaths. When she was a child, her parents were killed in a bus accident on their way to a wedding. Later on, both her sisters were widowed, like herself, and one of them died recently, as did the grandfather who had raised them all. . . .

It is not easy going over all this with the mother, who acts depressed and hostile. But she becomes particularly reticent when asked for more specific information about the death of her husband, Celeste's stepfather, a few years earlier. She say that she herself became "very ill", stricken by depression; then she mentions a civil suit that she had to bring against her in-laws over her husband's property in Africa, a suit that she says she lost—though she was able to keep the children, at least until now.

As for Celeste, her behaviour during this initial visit is completely discouraging. She is so reticent that she will not recount any subjective experience whatsoever and refuses all our attempts to arrive at a better understanding of her own history. Nor does she seem willing to make any investment in our day-hospital programme, or in any of the activities we propose. To my colleague from the medical-psychological centre I can only respond that Celeste's application to the day hospital seems premature, in view of her present inability to make any investment in it, and that for now it would be best for her to continue the participation she started at his centre, since she seems to have been going there willingly for the past few months. I also suggest that a stay in a full-time hospital be attempted over the summer, in order to make a "break", but the mother categorically rejects the idea of being separated from her daughter.

I see Celeste again a little before the summer vacation. She has now been expelled from her school and her symptoms have intensified to the point where she has broken off all contact. She stares fixedly, absently, into space and speaks a vaguely allusive discourse redolent with hostile fear. Her mother speaks of episodes of nocturnal restlessness and of anorexia; she says that Celeste spends long periods of time in front of the mirror, gazing silently at herself. The mother is now alarmed enough to accept a prescription of neuroleptics, and she no longer opposes a trial hospitalization. A bit more trusting now, she tells me that for a while now she has had a new life partner who has been very nice to the children and wants to help them. He wishes to marry her, and the two younger children are already calling him *"Daddy"*. But Celeste just calls him *"Uncle"*.

In the autumn I learn that Celeste was able to be hospitalized in a psychiatric ward for six weeks. The ordeal of separation prompts the mother to express fears of the possibility that her daughter is being experimented on "the way they do with African people". She is also afraid that she is not being told the truth about Celeste's condition, that perhaps it is serious or even incurable. She clearly associates her daughter's condition with her deceased husband's mysterious illness. But the hospitalization has at least enabled Celeste to resume normal eating and sleeping habits, a slight dose of neuroleptics having calmed her fears. Now conditions seem more favourable for establishing a therapeutic contract with us. I suggest that she come to our day hospital on a part-time basis, in order for her capacity for investment to be evaluated.

During her first weeks half-time at the day hospital she displays a striking passivity, with a pronounced tendency towards acting only under orders from our team—the way she acts at home, where she is dominated even by her little sister. She gives the impression that one could command her to do anything. In the course of our exchanges with her, we are struck by how Celeste appears to lose her bearings, especially with regard to time. We notice that especially where any sort of *starting point* or *origin* is concerned, everything becomes vague for her: her entry into elementary school, her entry into middle school, and so on (her entry into life...).

By the beginning of winter, her initial anxious panic has disappeared, but she still refrains from existing, suspending both actions and speech. She settles for merely observing what is happening around her, without getting further involved. At this point, I decide to propose a more systematic procedure to her mother for meetings between the team and the family, one particularly aimed at a better understanding of temporal and historical references. I also suggest that an African colleague belonging to the *Yoruba* tradition (South Benin) participate in these meetings.

The first meeting will leave us with the impression of a sort of "double-or-nothing". The mother brings along a young cousin whom she has taken under her roof. Celeste maintains her reserve completely, while her mother, still very reticent, offers the minimum by way of clarification, especially concerning the circumstances of her first husband's death. Despite her ill humour, she will nevertheless provide us with several keys to understanding. First, she asserts her repudiation of African tradition, of what she calls the "animist" explanations that try to give meaning to events—in particular, of course, to certain deaths. Not until the end of the conversation does she inform us that she belongs to the cult known as the *Celestial Christians* which effectively dictates a categorical rejection of all the traditional African rituals: "Everything that's not in the Bible," she says, "we reject."

We will part in an atmosphere of tension, left with the feeling that the mother wishes to break the therapeutic contract, refusing the terms that we have set. So I will be surprised to see, in the coming weeks, striking progress in Celeste's participation in the outpatient programme: she decides to make a painting on silk in the art studio, and her picture is not childish, as her regressive–

aggressive attitude might have led one to expect. She also begins to hover around my office door, obviously looking for opportunities to speak briefly with me.

One month later, the mother returns to meet with us, bringing Desiré, the psychotic little brother. He will do his utmost, after his own fashion, to monopolize a lot of attention; nevertheless, we manage to overcome the ordeal of the previous session, mainly by way of an explanatory review of the interpretations that the Celestial Christians (about which our African colleague is, fortunately, very well-informed) gave of her husband's death. His death is said to have been caused by a neurological disease, characterized by aphasia and paralysis, but it was interpreted by fellow cult members as a form of punishment—and his widow was forbidden to accompany her husband's body to the cemetery, lest she, too, be stricken with paralysis! . . . We take the opportunity to express (in Celeste's presence) the virulence of the cult's interpretations, which blocked the necessary mourning process—for the widow in the first place, of course, but also for Celeste, who was very attached to this "daddy".

After this very illuminating session, Celeste begins to participate actively, and not without talent, in a singing class, and she begins individual psycho-pedagogical work in French.

At the next session, Celeste's mother introduces us to her new husband. They both arrive at the day hospital all dressed up and offer us donuts. She is sporting a new African hairstyle; he is wearing a very elegant suit and tie. They express their gratitude for the progress that Celeste has made. We will be able to deal calmly with the family history in its totality, from the longstanding mystery of Celeste's biological father, to the very recent remarriage when, through some strange administrative error, the Christian name of Celeste's new stepfather was recorded on the certificate in the place of his African surname, thus becoming the new couple's *de facto* surname.

We now think it possible to suggest that Celeste enter the day hospital on a full-time basis, as her symptoms have lost the staggering traumatic characteristics that were in evidence earlier, and she is much more available. Moreover, she has manifested remarkable capacities for school work, as well as for music and dance.

Her mother will soon conceive another baby, which Celeste

will later be able to care for, thus regaining her role of big sister in the family group. At this time Celeste realizes that she is the same age that her mother was at the time of her own conception.

The team–family meetings will be interrupted for one year, while the mother dedicates herself to the new baby (and Celeste's psychologist–referent also happens to have gone on maternity leave at this time!).

One year later, after the birth of little Michael, we will review the remarkable progress of Celeste, who is now rather lively. But the mother gives us to understand that problems remain with her new in-laws, who have sent "emissaries" from Africa to observe the new household, apparently in order to understand how a 40-year-old woman saddled with three children—two of them psychotic—managed to get her hands on such a handsome young man.

This ordeal will last all autumn, and pressure from his family will convince Celeste's stepfather to stop meeting with us. We also notice that a certain blockage still remains in Celeste's ability to *question* her teachers when she does not understand something, and even to carry out simple research, such as looking up a word in the dictionary. Her French teacher tries to *shake her up* by declaring that this is an effect of the fuzziness about her origins, as though there were some kind of prohibition against clarifying anything, even the cause of her father's death.

The next day the mother storms into the hospital, furiously demanding to know why the teacher said such a thing. I seize the opportunity to see her twice by herself, along with my African colleague. But this will finally allow her to produce intelligible discourse about some obscure elements of their history. We then have the impression that we are witnessing the flowering of mythic speech *conceived* (found–created?) by her in order to resolve the difficulties she is struggling with.

She tells us, first of all, that the obstacles between her and the in-laws have been removed, that they now accept her, with Michael, and that she and her family plan to pay the in-laws in Africa a protocol visit just as soon as they can afford the trip. Later on, when her husband has started participating in our monthly meetings again, the mother will be able to revisit her African origins in an effective way, in order explain how Celeste's patronymic, despite coming from Celeste's biological father's side, nevertheless expresses allegiance to the mother's dead husband, because it also happens to be the name of the latter's grandfather (who was probably from the same clan as the biological father). Celeste is obviously relieved to hear this, and she forcefully asserts that she considers herself to be the eldest "daughter" of the dead man.

But his death still remains a mystery. The mother will tell us that in fact, she believes he was poisoned by his own family, during a meal. She says his brothers would have wanted to get him out of the way because his activities as a journalist for the opposition party were bad for their business. The attack of paralysis occurred right after a family banquet and is supposed to have been diagnosed as being a result of poisoning, but the family did not want to pursue an investigation. . . . After such a story, worthy of a Greek tragedy, the mother and children never went back to that place; and the question remains: how will their next visit go? Is there a possible solution? The mother declares (in front of Celeste) that one of the dead man's three children might *pay* for that renewal of family ties *with his or her life*. . . . The threat having been uttered, we will be able to continue its elaboration with Celeste, who will gradually overcome the inhibitions that have kept her from thinking and expressing herself. We will devote the last family therapy session of the year to Celeste's plans for professional training after she leaves the day hospital.

This observation over the course of three years seems to me to show how necessary it is, in cases dominated by a traumatic type of reaction, characterized by a pain-avoiding rejection of an incomprehensible reality, to create within the family and the hospital team *a containing speech matrix*, conducive to the shared activity of putting into words. Celeste's capacity for symbolization seems to have been overloaded by an effect of condensation, between the threat tied to the death of her journalist stepfather, the unclear circumstances of her own procreation, and the disappearance of her biological father. The establishment of a contract of minimal trust with the mother no doubt created the conditions for the establishment of a *shared speech area*, which could recover (create?) a plausible version of devastating events.

For Celeste, our programme of team–family meetings seemed

to have the *"matrix"* function, and the *transitional* function, of conferring an endurable meaning on events that had been merely endured, without meaning. I think this is essential for the traumatized patient: the weaving of a mythic discourse capable of giving meaning to the impact of traumatic events. We also note that, in this case (as in many cases of adolescents with delusional parents), making speech out of the "delusion" (the cult's and the parent's) within the context of convivial meetings and in the presence of the teenager enabled the latter to emerge from a state of confusion that was keeping her from effective participation in the activities proposed to her.

It is as if the experience's traumatic character were linked to the fact that the youngster is prevented from attaining understanding of existential information through an exchange of speech between generations, because the sources of meaning have not been placed at his/her disposition.

Clearly, in such cases, we cannot expect a young patient's speech to provide us with the keys for understanding and resolving what is making him/her suffer—as we usually can when dealing with neurotic disorders marked by the mechanism of repression. Here we are dealing with a deficiency in the capacity for symbolization; and this deficiency is obviously linked in part to capacities for psychic binding in the parents' generation. *Indeed, the traumatic experience generally proves to be chiefly that of the parents themselves,* from whom the youngster receives messages that strongly dissuade him/her from asking any questions.

It is therefore first of all from the parents that one must obtain an acceptance of participating to restore the conditions for a *discourse matrix*, holding enough meaning for vital exchanges and communication.

This leads us back to the idea that something can only be traumatic for a youngster if it is traumatic for his/her parents—in other words, if it overwhelms the parents' capacity for mental binding and, by the same token, the establishment of the reference points the youngster will need to subjectivate the events of his own life.

Unfortunately there are many cases where such a traumatic wound in the parents will prove to be insurmountable—kept out of reach by a *persistent disavowal* that forms a defensive narcissistic cover invalidating symbolization. Our therapeutic attempts to advance the suffering youngster's process of subjectivation must then use as a principal tool *the direct involvement of the therapists' psyches*—which often takes the form of acted repetition, and in a way that can often be very trying.

Notes

1. I was pleased to discover a convergence with Peter Blos, Jr (Detroit, Michigan) on this point.
2. As Philippe Gutton has so pertinently pointed out (1991).
3. We should relate this idea to Freud's at first surprising idea in *Group Psychology and the Analysis of the Ego* (1921c) that the child carries out a proto-identification to his father, perhaps at the same time he makes his first libidinal investment in his mother.
4. I have dealt with several cases where the father of the family "discovers" he is homosexual at the moment when his child is going through adolescence (which the father had been unable to experience).
5. "Blue helmets" is the usual expression for UN peacekeepers. [*Translator's note.*]

CHAPTER SIX

Foreclosure of signification and the suffering subject

The existence of established fantasy, a constructed *scenario* in the psychic apparatus, should not be taken for granted; it is not a *natural* given. Freud calls our attention to this in the first phase of "A Child Is Being Beaten" (1919e), as we saw in chapter 3. In our analytic practice, whether in our private office or in an institution, we are not always faced with a *fantasy transference* (more usually called *object transference*) in the patient. The phenomenon of displacement [*Übertragung*] of the past into the present which makes up the *transference* can in fact take place in very different registers; so that the gamut of said transferences constitutes a wide qualitative spectrum, based on the degree of symbolization and more basically the extent to which they can be *represented* in images in the patient's psyche.

This should remind us of the importance of *the real as a psychic category* (Lacan). This may be conceived of as a register of perceptive imprints that fall short of the possibility of being put into images in the psyche, and also as a residue of the process of symbolization. It is a register of the psychic apparatus, which should not as such be equated with the world's brute reality, which is the object of physicists, nor can it be limited to biological elements.

The phenomenon of the transference in the register of perceptive traces is related to repetition compulsion [*Wiederholungszwang*], where a *subject of fantasy* has not acquired existence. It is precisely our task as analysts to make this kind of transference *representable*, and by the same token "*subjectivable*" by the patient. Traumatic imprints have the power to reproduce themselves in present reality, depending on the case, and this power attains even greater compulsive force when the imprints are deprived of psychic imagery.

Freud wisely characterized delusion as an attempt at *restitution* [*Wiederherstellung*][1] involving something that has *already happened*—"a fragment of historical truth"—that has been insufficiently mentalized—"a lost piece of a lived history" (Freud, 1937d). Here he seems to be referring specifically to perceptive imprints that lack psychic binding, a defect that determines their traumatic potential.

Such psychic lacunae often come from a "default imprint", as Jean-Claude Arfouilloux[2] points out—due to parental messages that have taken the form of *disavowal* (of signification). In any case, the repetition compulsion inherent in this sort of perceptual imprint proves to be even more constraining and unavoidable when the patient has failed to put them into representations and involves him/herself with them in a constructed fantasy. Their repeated re-actualization then takes place either through the patient's own comportment, or through bodily experiences or somatic manifestations, or through the ever-startling "*repetition induced in the other*" (the therapist in particular), to which we will return.

The difficult work of the subjective appropriation of such an already-happened-not-truly-experienced (Winnicott) which insistently returns leads to an interest in *ghostly* phenomena (Penot 1996). We know that ghosts are traditionally associated with the necessity of re-establishing some truth that has been banished (by a *disavowal* of judgement); so, the apparition will keep compulsively coming back until the fact whose meaning has been abolished can be restored, by a process of acknowledgement, of *restitution*.

The therapist grappling with this sort of *ghostly return* (in the form of a delusion, for example) will observe that there are indeed different types of countertransference. The experience will allow the therapist to measure the gap between what he or she usually understands as "countertransference" in the strict sense—that is, his or her subjective reaction to the fantasy projection carried out on him or her by the patient (to which the therapist has lent him/herself), and a completely different kind of involvement. At the other extreme of transference actualization, in fact, the most experienced analyst can find him/herself caught against his or her will in the "repetition induced in the other"—in such a way that his or her very perceptions are taken captive.

Psychoanalytic teamwork

This sort of phenomenon is easier to spot when we are able to *work psychoanalytically as a team* (Penot, 2005)—in psychodrama, for example, or in an institution organized for psychoanalytic teamwork. We are then able to observe, through our elaboration in the *clinical synthesis*, or team meeting, a set of divergent attitudes that, we have reason to believe, reproduce certain characteristic relationships within the patient's original milieu, keeping them from attaining meaning, and therefore being subjectively appropriated, through a process of *disavowal–splitting*. Seeing such radically divergent, indeed incompatible, attitudes in a group of colleagues who have worked well together for a long time allows us to grasp the *uncanniness* of what is happening *among* the therapists who are in contact with certain patients—especially since these clashing attitudes do not necessarily correspond to the usual personalities of those who exhibit them. A minimal overview of the patient's treatment history will regularly reveal that he/she has been implicated in a repetitive series (sometimes a long one) of such relational impasses, with all sorts of different protagonists.

The lack of mutual identification that prevails at such times among caregivers will have to be borne by them and worked on (worked through) for a long time, producing a kind of developed reproduction of the *splittings* (the *schize*) imprinted in the psyche of the patient in question, which hamper subjectivation in him/her. I cannot stress enough the interest of simultaneously also working with the family, in order to obtain a certain verification of the clues to such lacunae in relationships and in the process of representation, with the disavowal that usually underlies them. Then the therapeutic team can perceive that that is the location of a *transference of disavowal*, from the case it is dealing with.

I should explain why I prefer to avoid using the term *"projection"* here, or even *"projective identification"*, to describe the kind of transference we are dealing with as a team. It is because I think that words in themselves carry implicit representations—even, I would say, an implicit philosophy. The term *projection* cannot help but suggest an *imaginary process*, while it is my conviction that the phenomenon I am talking about is mainly the result of a *lack* of mental imagery, more precisely of organized fantasy in the patient's psyche.

The mechanism of projective identification was introduced by Melanie Klein in 1946. However, she envisioned it as the projection of a fantasy intolerable for the patient's ego into the psyche of the therapist. Fortunately, many "post-Kleinian" authors, such as Herbert Rosenfeld and Betty Joseph, have considerably transformed the content of that notion of projective identification.

Bion probably went furthest in redefining it, and I think his theoretical line converges more (even using other terms) with the one I am proposing here on the basis of other sources. Notably, when Bion speaks of "undigested parts of [the patient's] experience" (1967), he is obviously speaking of what I call perceptual traces (prints) lacking of mental representation. A common perspective is to consider projective identification not only as a defence in the service of (egoical) mis-recognition, but also as a way of experiencing something that requires (and pushes towards) more mental representation.

I shall illustrate what I am saying with the treatment of another adolescent in our day hospital. This treatment, involving several team members, essentially turned around a *foreclosure* of certain signifiers, which invalidated the subject himself. We had to carry out a treatment at the very roots of subjectivation, at a moment when individual psychotherapy did not yet seem possible for this patient.[3]

I hope that the deductive nature of this work will not seem too scabrous to the reader, and that it will be spared the fate of *rejection*, which has been the psychoanalytic milieu's defensive reflex ever since Freud's made his valiant attempt to write about *telepathy* (1921c).

The case of "Angel"

I first received this boy at the age of 14, when he arrived at our hospital with a label of "entry into schizophrenia" and a prescription for Haldol. He had been adopted at the end of his first year by a bourgeois Parisian couple, when it appeared that the husband's low sperm count would prevent them from ever having a baby. Something in the circumstances of this psychotic breakdown in adolescence struck me right away: it seems to have followed the unexpected discovery of jaundice due to Gilbert's disease, a benign congenital liver condition. The teenager had then begun to manifest an intense anxiety of depersonalization, with psychotic overtones, and became extremely aggressive and rejecting towards his adoptive parents. He was expelled from his school, and quickly refused by another, before coming to our institution, where he would be treated for three years. I wondered about the strangely destabilizing power of the congenital "stigma"—a sudden re-apparition, in the present, of his biological parents (real, yet unknown, in a sense *abolished*), a "signifier" of something in the boy's biological origin.

His adoptive mother, very much the homemaker, kept insisting: "For me, it's exactly as if I had given birth to him. . . ." Striving to reconstitute her son's early childhood for me, irreproachable medical records in hand, she said that though a very beautiful baby, he was "perhaps a little stiff, tense". The father then chimes in with, "he was suspicious!" This remarkable movement of *projective identification* hints at an adoptive parent's own suspicious gaze upon this "seed" sprung from who-knows-where (a suspicion that had found confirmation in the appearance of the congenital stigma?)

Another example of the father's basically projective attitudes was provided by his remarks about some right-wing extremist views expressed by the son: "He has pretty radical ideas about his fellow human beings. If it were up to him, there'd be fewer people on Earth!" said this infertile man.

Once he was admitted to our day hospital, this handsome boy would show himself to be more perverse than schizophrenic. I will call him "Angel", after the ambiguous, seductive angel in Pasolini's film *Teorema*.

I cannot develop in this work all the ins and outs of the psychoanalytic teamwork we had to carry out with him over the course of three years. Suffice it to say that we had mainly to overcome the destructive effects of *incompatible feelings* that arose among the team members who were in contact with this strange boy. Everyone's experiences tended to be mutually exclusive, along the lines of a mutual *disqualification* or *disavowal*, and this within a team that had been working rather well together for a long time.

No subject seemed to result from the rift, the sort of *disavowal–splitting*, that divided the boy's referent caregivers—each no doubt caught up in the impossibility of emerging as a subject in the face of a certain non-response from his or her counterpart.

Only during Angel's second year of hospitalization did his psychologist–referent begin to overcome her "embarrassment" enough to be able to verbalize in our clinical synthesis the uneasiness she was prey to when she found herself alone in a room with Angel. She said that she would then feel in danger of fainting, of blacking out, that her thinking was completely baffled. It is noteworthy that at such times she never even thought of calling out to colleagues within earshot. This reminds me of what Freud says about the childhood experience of the "Wolf Man" (1918b [1914]), who was hallucinating that his finger had been severed and yet could not call out to his Nanny, who was close by.

So there seemed to be something unnameable, impossible to formulate, that had to be lived through. The violence of such an experience was all the more striking in that it involved a seasoned psychologist, who was also a former nurse. In addition, there was a striking contrast between her feelings and the attitudes of other female team members towards Angel: another psychologist willingly let him nuzzle up against her neck, certain that this behaviour was simply the innocent manifestation of a little boy who, she said, "didn't get enough cuddling". But others did not like having to witness such scenes, which they found "perverse".

The male team members were also divided into violently clashing, incompatible subjective positions. Angel's educator–referent complained of feeling constantly disavowed—"*couillonné*" was the word he kept using (a mildly vulgar expression meaning "to be made a fool of", but whose literal connotations refer to the testicles, or "balls"). Another male colleague, however, used to speak of his "positive relationship" with this boy, who moved him to solicitude.

We know how sometimes a virulent imaginary disavowal of the biological parents can prevail in the minds of troubled adoptive parents. This state of mind (especially when it is "unconscious") tends to have a destructive, de-narcissizing effect on the adopted child, whose narcissistic references may boomerang between the "nasty abandoners" and the "child-stealers". It seems as though adoptive parents may have even more reason to blacken the hypothetical image of the biological parents (the "real" parents, as they are bizarrely called) when they are having trouble exercising their own parental function.

Our psychoanalytic teamwork concentrated on mentalizing these difficult feelings and the "impossible" relationships they tend to create between team members, laboriously putting them into words for ourselves, representing them—hypothetically, of course, in the sense of what Freud calls *constructions in the analysis* (1937d).

One day in the synthesis, Angel's psychologist–referent finally expressed, not without anger and resentment, that in her work with Angel, she felt like "a woman without enough protection". She was then able to realize the extent to which she had found herself locked into the probable experience of the ghostly, unknown biological mother—as if she were the *Dibbuk*[4] of a real being that has been abolished, leaving no words or image—in other words, *foreclosed*. As it turned out, our psychologist was not the only person who had had to reprise the role of "woman without enough protection": at the very end of Angel's treatment, his mother would reveal during a family session, and thus *in Angel's presence*, of course, that he had physically battered her at the time of his breakdown. She had never breathed a word of this to her husband.

As a result of the process of mentalization going on around him, Angel gradually managed to improve his behaviour, and to develop a rather rich fantasy life, inventing a private family romance about an Anglo–Saxon origin (made plausible by his sandy hair and freckles.) He insisted on adopting an English nickname, "Bad luck". Which makes one wonder: bad luck for whom? For himself, because of the way he'd turned out? For his biological parents, because they could not take responsibility for him? For his adoptive parents, because they were dealt such a bad hand? For us, finally, because we had to deal with this very trying case? . . .

Then Angel ran away from home to London, where he managed to live on his own for a week (establishing contact with his father by telephone). He came back expressing his satisfaction at having accomplished something "personal", and he was able to return more successfully to his secondary studies.

I happened to see this young man again, several years later. He came to ask me some questions about fatherhood, for, at 25, he who was supposed to have wished there were "fewer people on Earth" already had a large family to take care of—two children and two stepchildren. . . .

A transference of the psychic real?

This therapeutic history can give one an idea of the repetition compulsion the therapists find themselves caught up in, as soon as they attempt to *take charge* of such a case. It is as if a certain deficiency in thing-representations and primary thought processes comes to be concretized in their own-persons, transported by the patient.

A transference of this order mainly tends to take behavioural forms, which attest to an inability to metaphorize what is at stake—that is, a *dis-placement* of it onto other(s) without more manageable supports for representation. In practice, the therapist can grasp the nature of his or her involvement in this kind of transference only *after the fact* ("*après-coup*") and in a deductive way, as if the determinism in question short-circuited his or her own (pre-conscious) system of representations. But such cases are not limited to psychiatric institutions, and the lone psychoanalyst in private practice can also be exposed to this phenomenon, probably more often than he or she usually thinks; for the lack of confrontation with others that is characteristic of private practice makes it even more likely that he or she will remain unaware of the fundamental *partiality* of his or her position.

And yet these configurations of disavowal are indeed the only kind of transference certain patients are capable of—an obligatory and necessary revisiting of their matrix (proto-parental) constellation and of the non-response that holds them in suspense, indefinitely. This *real imprint* in the form of a lacunae in representation constitutes the passage of working through (perlaboration) required for the emergence of any "subject of the id".

I propose that, with such cases, the interpretative work must be applied to the problem of subjectivation of the therapist him/herself, the establishment of this *exterior proto-subject* Freud (1915c) is speaking about (chapter 1).[5] Winnicott (1963) was the first to provide illustrations of this, with regard to defects in the *setting*: the defects in the other-therapist that re-actualize some deficiency in the protagonists who presided at the patient's birth as a subject. We are often alerted to this by the *disqualifying/invalidating* relationship established among colleagues working with a certain patient—or even between the analyst and military police officers in a case described by Louise de Urtubey (1994).

When there is such a degree of (mutual) alienation in the transference, interpretation must not be directed to the patient at first. It can only be received and understood by him/her after we have sufficiently suspended our *attributive judgement* (Freud, 1925h). Beforehand, the therapist will have to acknowledge, by elucidating it with others, the unexpected role of *new subject* (Freud, 1915c) that he or she has shouldered against his or her will within the repetition compulsion. This acknowledgement by the protagonist can open the way towards a putting into images and into words hitherto inaccessible to the patient and can allow the latter to appropriate for his/her own use new tools of mental (subjective) representation.

A story like Angel's helps us to conceive of the *foreclosing* effects of a certain kind of defence coming from the parents: a narcissistic defence in the mode of *disavowal*, which manifests itself particularly in a tendency towards projection that can mortgage in a lasting way their child's process of subjectivation. Above all, we see that this kind of narcissistic defence essentially consists of rejecting the very meaning of what should have been perceived as a *referential lack* (the parent's sterility, for example, or the congenital mark of jaundice), by the same token invalidating the particular subject who should have been produced in the process.

What is a signifier?

Some schizophrenic adolescents can provide an opportunity for observing that certain word-representations carried by their discourse hold no usable meaning for them but, rather, give rise only to an *uncanny* feeling.

This was notably the case of an older boy preparing for his baccalaureate exam, in whose typically schizophrenic speech I could make out, among other things, the strange statement: "*Creil is near Pau . . .*" (two very distant French towns). When this geographically untenable statement was reported to his parents, they just laughed scornfully and said, "Well, you know perfectly well that he's nuts!"

But it so happened that I was fortunate enough to be contacted shortly thereafter by "an old family friend", from whom I was astonished to learn that these two towns, Creil and Pau, were none other than respective places of residence of his maternal grandfather and the maternal grandmother's lover (i.e., the "old family friend" himself)!

At the next meeting with the family, I was able to verify that these toponymic signifiers still had for the patient's mother the status of raw, traumatic material. As a little girl in 1944, in the railway station at Creil, with the bombs falling all around, she had been sent away by her recently divorced father who refused to take her in, considering that it was not his legal visitation day! So the relation between the two signifiers, Creil and Pau, barred in the mother's mind, produced no subjectivation in this boy (who was not mentally deficient—he incidentally received a top mark in his examination in French literature).

These words, probably spoken in front of the boy by a slightly "mad" old aunt, could *not work as* signifiers for him; they were bits of *psychic real* taken *"en masse"* from his mother's traumatic experience. Their signifying foreclosure was no doubt maintained by the mother because of the unliveable (unnameable) character of the drama they harked back to—a true rejection of fatherhood, which, I later learned, had followed upon another kind of disavowal of the father's name: the abolition, by the paternal grandmother, of the family's Russian-sounding patronymic.

Here we should point out a fundamental fact: *nothing is a signifier in itself.* Lacan never gave any definition but a subjective one to the signifier—a signifier exists only in relation to a subject for another signifier (1960b, p. 676). This disconcerting formula suggests something like a synchronous mutating emergence: one representation can only acquire signifying value in relation to others, on the one hand, and to a subject, on the other. The result is that one cannot conceive of a signifier without subjectivity, any more than one could conceive of a signifier in isolation. This calls to mind hypotheses about the appearance of language on Earth, which many consider could only have happened *all at once.* For signifier and subject must determine each other within a synchronous interaction, and we will have occasion to return to this necessary reciprocity at work in the very process of subjectivation, wherein the drive interaction must be restarted by successive signifying responses from the protagonists.

The starting "model" of this can be found in the first interactions between mother and baby. The newborn's first appeals (cries . . .) are perceived as *significant* by the mother, appealing to her behavioural response. At this point, such a response represents the *subject–mother* in relation with the *signifier* newborn manifestation. But soon afterwards, this model alters: the newborn's reaction (mimics, gestures . . .) will represent *the nascent subject* in relation with the mother's signifying manifestation. And so on. The subjectivizing machinery has begun to function, for better or for worse. . . .

It is rather curious that Lacan remained fascinated for a large part of his theoretical career by the idea of the "signifier in itself"— the "pure signifier", and so forth—when this kind of objectifying notion is fundamentally incompatible with the definition he himself proposes. Such a paradox recalls the nostalgia that Freud expressed for a psychoanalysis that would be objectified in such a way as to finally figure among the Natural Sciences—when the genius of the Freudian approach is that it revealed the laws proper to subjective determinism. . . .

In his discussion of my report (Penot, 1999a), Daniel Widlöcher (1999) recalled the famous case of the stele found in the desert, covered with weird signs. The discoverer thinks that these must be *signifiers*, more or less hieroglyphic in appearance. But of their meaning he has, in sum, only a notion. These signs cannot really play the role of signifiers for him, because he does not have the subjective key.

Such an experience echoes what clinical work shows us about the relation that certain psychotics have with signifiers that have been abolished as such (*foreclosed*), with the notion that they represent something undoubtedly important in the prehistory of their subjectivity. These patients can suspect (and one can remind them) that it *should* mean something to them (because it does for us) and that they should react subjectively. . . . But they cannot do this; at most they can experience these signs as confusedly persecutory and uncanny—*it's all Greek to me,* as one says.

Approaching psychosis with an analyst's rigor should imply, above all, that one takes the subjective relativity of the signifier into account. A psychoanalytic approach that ignores this fundamental fact is liable to *alienate* these patients even more—and this was unfortunately what happened when psychoanalytic technique was first *applied*[6] to psychosis.

Scientificity and psychoanalytic approach

The intrinsic bond between the signifier and the subjective raises an essential question: how can an approach aimed at the *subjective* claim to be "scientific", in the modern sense of being objectively verifiable and reproducible? Though Freud long cherished the idea that psychoanalysis might some day figure among the natural sciences, Lacan hesitated a great deal before considering that the discourse of science fundamentally implied an *abolition of the subject* as such—primarily, of course, the *subject of the statement* that interests the psychoanalyst more than anything, since it bears the preconscious intentional motion.

Scientific discourse's tendency to abolish the subject can be observed in the field of what are called the *human* (and therefore *soft*) *sciences*—where *statistical* truth tends to hold a place, leading to the pseudo-objectivity of survey results and their systematic use in abolishing subjective responsibility in (political) decisions.

This is also what characterizes psychological approaches based on *conditioning*: pure applications of the "master's (the boss's) discourse", which Lacan characterizes as representing "the other side of psychoanalysis" (1969–1970). The tendency of modern techniques to make the very dimension of the subject disappear can feed into the idea that psychoanalysis could have arisen, at the dawn of the twentieth century, as a sort of antidote to the generalization of the new-scientificity-whose-effect-is-to-abolish-subjective-error. From this perspective, the specific mission of psychoanalysis would be to set itself up as the investigative method *par excellence* of human subjectivity, its positivist attitude nevertheless conferring a certain "scientificity" upon it, in comparison to various spiritualist approaches.

Regarding the scientific spirit of "modernity", one must also note the enduring distrust exhibited by Lacan (at least until the early 1970s) towards the register of formal representation—what he calls the category of the *imaginary*.[7] In this we can see a manifestation in him of a "modernist" state of mind, with maximum credit given to *languages* (especially those of computer science) and, in the final analysis, to mathematical language itself. For it is a fact that such reluctance with regard to the truth of *imaginary representations* was absolutely not characteristic of the thinkers of the Renaissance, or of the twelfth century, and even less of the ancient Greeks. Something happened in the Modern period (especially since Descartes) and was further radicalized in the second half of the twentieth century with the telecommunications boom, making the method of the physical sciences more and more exclusive of any approach that proposed to take into account the conditions of the exercise of subjectivity.

A necessary return to Aristotle

An Israeli author, Yeshayahou Leibowitz (1987), sheds precious light on this subject. Among other things, he seeks to make more explicit the present paradox of the so-called human sciences. He starts with the observation that there has been a real mutation in the modern scientific approach concerning the very notion of *causality*; indeed, he believes that this has been considerably reduced within what is now considered as a "scientific" approach.

A brief review may be useful here. First Leibowitz revisits some fundamental considerations posited by Maïmonides in his famous *Guide for the Perplexed* (the "misfits"!), where he treats the relation between the concepts of *true* and *false*, on the one hand, and those of *good* and *evil* on the other.

On this point, Leibowitz thinks, "the dividing line does not separate believers and unbelievers, it crosses each camp and turns around the question: is it possible to associate these notions?" (p. 42)

The French mathematician Henri Poincaré already judged (in 1905) that "morality and science have their own domains which [touch] but don't penetrate each other". More precisely: "One shows us what goal we should aim, for the other, once the goal has been given, shows us the means of reaching it. They can thus never run contrary to each other, since they cannot meet." And he concludes: "There can be no immoral science, any more than there could be a scientific morality."

But it is in relation to the ideas of Aristotle—the basic reference of every scientific approach since the dawn of what we call "modern times"—that one can gauge the extent to which things have come to be posited in completely different terms today. Aristotle had posited as a general rule that "to understand something is to know the causes of that thing". Now it is exactly on the notion of cause that our modernity has radically changed the givens of this problem. Aristotle had, in fact, distinguished four orders of causes:

1. First, what he called the "material cause", the very matter of which the thing is made—the way a table is made of wood, for example. But we immediately see that this is insufficient causality to explain the existence of said table—that a *transforming*

agent was also necessary, to transform the wooden material, using appropriate means.

2. Therefore the carpenter (with his means) represents the "efficient cause" of the table's existence. But for Aristotle this is still not enough: for nothing obliges the carpenter to act. In order to understand the existence of this table, we must therefore presuppose that carpenter has the *intention* to make it.
3. This intentionality is what Aristotle calls "the final cause".

But these three causalities—material, efficient, and final—still are not enough, and Aristotle considers that a fourth factor must be added to these three necessary factors.

4. It is the *image* (model) that the carpenter has in his mind when he constructs the table. Aristotle calls this the "formal cause". So we see that, like a good ancient Greek, he thus elevates the formal representation (what Lacan called the imaginary) to the rank of a causal factor.

Of course, Aristotle intended to apply his causal categories to the whole of the so-called natural sciences. In him this came from a general philosophical conception that included the conviction that each thing existing in nature should have its finality—that is, it should have a sort of *intentionality* behind it.

With this in mind, we can see how today's scientificity considers only one of these four registers as causal in the proper sense—that of the *efficient cause*—insofar as A makes necessary the existence of B; in order words, strictly *deductive* causality.

The materiality of an object is now considered only as a practical *condition* but not a cause (of the existence of the table); as for the formal cause, it only intervenes in the mind of the one who perceives the object, not in the object itself; lastly, the final cause has also been definitively excluded from the field of the natural sciences because it comes only from the subjective intentionality of man.

Of course, it is on this point that the essential part of what constitutes the psychoanalyst's approach hinges. For though it is undeniable that modern science has provided itself with increased efficiency thanks to this methodological constriction, psychoanalysis cannot follow the same path in hopes of attaining any rigor whatsoever in a practice that aims to understand the determinism proper to human subjectivity.[8]

In Aristotle's own terms, we can point out that the rigour of our own approach to subjective determinism cannot be reduced merely to the register of causality he calls *efficient*. The register of *final causes*, as well as that of *formal causes*, necessarily intervenes— and in a central way—in the determinism of psychic functioning, for the latter is described by Freud as intrinsically finalized, supported by what he calls the *"Zielvorstellung"*.[10]

It is a fact that the so-called human sciences, as soon as they strive to conform to the laws governing the natural sciences (which consider man as one of the *objects* of this same nature), confront the researcher with an ineluctable choice between two different approaches. Either one tries to hold with an experimental choice that conforms to the (objective) sciences of nature, making it impossible to take into account subjectivity as such; or one chooses an approach that aims at knowledge of this subjectivity, and it will then be necessary to integrate, as elements of causality, the aim-presentations that issue from unconscious desire. In this case, however, we must renounce any claim to a place among approaches that are "scientific" in the proper, limited sense.

It does seem that many psychoanalytic institutes throughout the world are not ready to undertake such a process of mourning—probably because they imagine that in so doing they would weaken the credibility of psychoanalysis, by removing it from the natural sciences' race towards scientific objectivity.

I shall conclude this brief discussion of scientificity by suggesting that the danger could also work the other way: that psychoanalysis most exposes itself to the danger of dying out when it strives to base itself on objective science—and also, on the other hand, when it seeks justification in philosophical discourse. These are both paths towards the loss of its own rigor: that which corresponds to its specific—subjective and unconscious—object.

The primary (objectivizing) threat hangs over the psychoanalytic institutes that are so careful to give a scientific appearance to their research programmes: isn't research into unconscious subjective determinism then in danger of simply being emptied out? The second (philosophical) path is illustrated by the recent success of a revisionist criticism like that of Borch-Jacobsen (2001). Many psychoanalysts in France have shown enthusiasm for him—at least as long as he seemed to be taking aim only at Lacan—until the moment of truth, when the *final cause* of his project was unveiled: to throw Freud out with the bath water. . . .[9]

Symbolization and absence

Accepting that the object of psychoanalytic work is essentially the *process of subjectivation* leads us to reconsider how this relies essentially on the work of *symbolization*. Here we must return to Freud's fundamental observation that one can only symbolize something if one can conceive of its absence (lost object). This ties in with the pivotal role of possible acknowledgement of the *lack* of the mother, insofar as it commands the chances for a developing subject to be able to situate itself within the sexual symbolic.

Let us say that the key precondition for the symbolic putting-into-play of a representation is that the possible absence of the object it represents be conceivable without too much narcissistic damage.[11]

In order to better define in this regard what a signifier is, and the key role it plays in subjectivation, I think it could be enlightening to revisit in the next chapter Lacan's view of the destiny of the emblematic figure of the *phallus* in psychic life. What becomes of this can indeed be considered exemplary insofar as it provides the best illustration of the qualitative mutation that enables an image to become fully functional as a signifier—in this case, to come to represent the possible absence inherent in sexual difference and, through this, desire, in such a way as to act as a major referent for a better subjectivation of play of the sexual drives.

Notes

1. Strachey translates *Wiederherstellung* as "cure", which I think is a mistake. I prefer to retain the word "restitution". See "Constructions in Analysis" (1937d), pp. 267–268.

2. Paper presented at the Journées Occitanes in Montpellier in November 1997 (Arfouilloux, 1997).

3. I first presented this rather striking therapeutic history in November 1990, at the meeting of the COPELFI in Jerusalem.

4. This ghostly return of a misunderstood dead person is well known in Cabbalistic tradition.

5. Xavier Jacquey (1975) was the first of us to speak of the *"subjectal position"* of the analyst in the transference.

6. It should be pointed out that the idea of the *application* of psychoanalysis is itself fallacious, for one notices that it is mainly at the limits of its own field that psychoanalysis learns the most and increases, or even rectifies, its theorization. This term *application* betrays a certain arrogance that tends to minimize what in fact constitutes what is the most creative in psychoanalytic research: the areas of its activity where it makes the most progress.

7. It is also important not to forget that the *formal regression* that makes up the representative system of the dream nevertheless translates in its way the symbolization acquired elsewhere in the psyche of the dreamer; in this it differs fundamentally from the hallucination of the psychotic, which is produced *in the absence of symbolization*. Also the signifying potential of the dream figurations will be able to be restored through the association of ideas, during waking hours, which is not possible with the delusion or hallucination of a psychotic nature.

8. A very careful clinical illustration has been proposed by our American colleague, Owen Renik (1998), concerning the subjectivity and objectivity of the analyst in the session.

9. François Roustang has followed a similar critical trajectory, finally arriving at . . . a rediscovery of hypnosis (!).

10. Literally "aim-presentation", rather than the phrase "purposive idea" chosen by Strachey (e.g., Freud, 1900a, 1950 [1895]). (See the entry "Purposive idea" in Laplanche & Pontalis, 1973, pp. 373–374.)

11. This why I have thought it necessary to begin with a re-examination of the question of *disavowal—of absence*. (Penot, 1989).

CHAPTER SEVEN

The key role of the *phallus* signifier in the subjectivation of sexuality

The phallus[1] (representation of the erect male organ) has had, throughout all times and in many different cultures, the function of representing human desire. But this representation is in itself the vehicle for a sort of intrinsic paradox whose *economic* incidence is illustrated by the case Freud reports of certain adults fixated on the imaginary representation of "the woman with a penis". There is a kind of freeze-frame effect in those who have the typical dream, wherein, Freud says (1908c): "the dreamer, in a state of nocturnal sexual excitation, will throw a woman down, strip her and prepare for intercourse—and then, in place of the female genitals, he beholds a well-developed penis and breaks off the dream and the excitation" (p. 216). Here the dreamer's awakening is a punishment for the dream's failure to provide a solution in terms of libidinal economy; it is as if the appearance of the erect penis was in itself traumatic, stopping dead the pursuit of the sexual aim and the search for drive satisfaction.

Disavowal of absence and invalidation of signification

We know that the disavowal of the absence of a penis in the woman was considered by Freud to be the prototype for the *disavowal of reality*. It seems that the recognition of the penis' absence is a source of violent displeasure, while the hallucinatory apparition of the erect penis in the dream woman is also traumatic. This kind of functional impasse should lead us to suspect that the representation of the phallus cannot be taken simply as the (partial) object of desire, but that it must acquire an *eminently mutative and paradoxical value* if it is to enable the psychic economy to overcome the trauma of sexual difference and allow the sexed subject to sustain itself as desiring.

As soon as he begins to give an account of infantile sexuality, Freud posits that the child usually goes through a *period of disavowal* (of what he can perceive), and that his way of overcoming this will determine the conditions of functional access to the genital phase. In the mean time, what Freud chooses to call the *"phallic phase"* is characterized in the little boy by an imaginary dominance of the phallic attribute associated with a search for masturbatory pleasure—which will in the girl be located in the clitoris, since she has not sensually located her vagina.

Lacan will radicalize Freud's argument by maintaining that we should start with the fact that the mother is first imagined as phallic by the child—whether the latter be male or female. As a result of this, he says, "the signification of castration takes on its effective weight with regard to the formation of symptoms only once it has been discovered as a castration of the mother" (1964). This initial tendency to represent the mother as having a phallus established itself as a basic element in Freud's discovery of the system of the Unconscious, made up of relatively stable elements that Freud chose to call *thing-representations*. One of Freud's principal discoveries from dreams (1900a) is that these thing-representations can form meaningful sequences, according to the process of the rebus.

From this other scene of the Unconscious come messages whose possible meaning Freud tried to decipher—in dreams, but also in the formation of neurotic symptoms. Regarding this, Lacan points out that this idea of a *discourse* emanating from the Unconscious cannot be taxed with any sort of culturalism (even less of idealism) since here it is not a matter of language as a verbal instrument of social exchange. I already evoked this notion when examining the concept of signifier at the end of the preceding chapter.

Now, among these thing-representations, that of the erect penis intervenes in an exemplary way in the particular mode of expression of the Unconscious system: the primary thought process. From a psychoanalytic perspective, the mental representation of the phallus cannot be considered the simple (static) image of a libidinal object—whether it be declared partial, internal, good, or bad; even less can it be equated with the real male organ, the penis, which it symbolizes ("This is not a pipe", as Magritte says!)

Lacan thinks that the phallus is called to play in the Unconscious neither more nor less than the role of a *signifier*, but a signifier that is especially privileged in the psychic economy. Why? If the representation of the phallus has always been at the centre of initiations, in Egypt, in Greece, and all the way to the Andes, it is undoubtedly because, as the image of the erect penis, it constitutes the most salient element of the real copulation of engenderment. It has always held a *symbolic* role, in the etymological sense of constituting one of the two parts of a *copula*, of an asymmetrical assemblage, complementary rather than specular (the male piece fits with the female piece). In addition, the universal place of the phallic representation is based on the penis' singular quality of *turgidity*—what Ernest Jones called its "aphanisis"—that is, its specific capacity for fading away, because its erection is intermittent. So the image of the erect penis has always represented, for both sexes, the crucial uncertainties of *being* and *having*.

What Lacan says here is interesting because it makes explicit the necessity of mutation in the signification of the phallus. The static image of the erect penis, a figure of completeness and smugness that Lacan calls *phi* (ϕ), ought in effect to evolve towards the symbolic status of representing desire, insofar as desire, on the contrary, implies the recognition of a *lack*—this is the function he calls *minus phi* ($-\phi$), of castration. The mental representation of the erect penis is thus called to lend itself to signify this paradox of desire, not only because of the intermittence of the penile erection, but also because of the visible absence of a penis in half the human beings in the world. It is thus precisely the *avowal* (the opposite of disavowal) of desire that the image of the phallus will represent, starting with the fact that the mother desires what she recognizes is lacking to her.

Going back now to the famous Lacanian definition of the signifier—*"a signifier represents a subject for another signifier"*—one could say that the phallus signifier will thus have the capacity to articulate itself with some signifier of the mother's lack to represent the subject of a desire. In this way the phallus comes to constitute a pivotal representation, emblematic of the parental other's submission to the order of symbolic exchange—that is, the *de-totalitarization* of this other, which is the precondition for the emergence of the subject of a desire.

The child's understanding of his mother's demand for love intervenes in a decisive way, not so much because it helps the child deduce whether or not he himself has a phallus, but because *"he thus learns that his mother lacks one, because she's asking for one"*. And these are precisely the preconditions for passing beyond the disavowal of the lack (in the mother, first of all) that will determine the different symptomatic forms that the castration complex can take, starting with phobia, as in the case of Little Hans (Freud, 1909b). It is incumbent upon the psychoanalyst to evaluate, in each case and at every dynamic moment of a treatment, the place of the phallus signifier through which, as it turns out, man and woman can be "played" differently (in the game of sexual desire).

From this perspective, we should be especially attentive to treatments of homosexuals, through which we can see particularly well how positional constraints of sexual choice will be played out in relation to the phallic representation. We know that male homosexuality is essentially polarized on the side of the effective mark in the partner of *having* the phallus. Therefore, the manifest presence of a penis (a fetish, halfway down the road to meaning) proves to be a necessary support for desire.

As for the female homosexual, she reveals herself to be much more anchored in the necessity of making up for the disappointment she feels at a father perceived as having failed to give her a phallic endowment:[2] a symbolic father–mother, phallus-bearing and not marked by impotence as the father of the hysteric is. So the father of the lesbian is idealized, imitated, and hated, all at once, which further reinforces in her the element of the demand for love from the other woman, as Freud understood in the case of his young lesbian patient (1920a).

The fact of having had several homosexual women in psychoanalysis in recent years prompted me to reinvestigate the singular and paradoxical evolution that must be achieved in the phallus representation to be put into play, with the sort of mutating reversal it must undergo in the process of the subject's emergence. We observe that it is chiefly by overcoming the difficulty of tolerating a certain *passivation* that such subjective development can be attained; and this is a trial that proves particularly problematic for female homosexuals.

The treatment of Nicole

I will now talk about the treatment of Nicole, who began her analysis at the age of 42. At that time she said she felt that she was at the end of something: "*at the end of a cycle*", as she put it. Her presentation was rather a caricature of the sort of lesbian popularly referred to as "butch": very much a "guy", short-haired, she had taken to picking up slightly lost young foreign women. It was when her last girlfriend returned to South America that she started to feel "*tired of this system*" where she was always in the active, dominant position, and began to imagine a relationship that could be "*more enriching*" for her. She also gives me to understand that her aging father's worsening state of health had played a decisive role in this critical self-examination.

Nicole grew up in a provincial city where her father directed a high-profile business. The eldest of three children, she had been designated as heir apparent to her father's business, in preference to her brother (two years her junior), who wasn't doing well in school. But around the age of 25, she did a sudden about-face: after going to business school, she suddenly broke with her family and her diplomat fiancé to go live in South America with a girlfriend, Victoire, who fascinated her with her audacity as a journalist. She describes Victoire as imperious and possessive, prone to temper tantrums that Nicole realizes are similar to ones her father had during her childhood. In fact, her transatlantic flight followed upon her discovery that the famous paternal business was bankrupt, its failure long hidden behind a grand façade. One might say that the paternal phallus then showed itself to her in its disappointing, illusory aspect.

Of course, the feeling of having been *hoodwinked* was a cardinal element noted by Freud in the case of the young homosexual woman (1920a): he points to the disappointment experienced by this girl who hoped to receive a phallus from the father—in this case, a baby of his.

I should mention that Nicole had adopted a baby boy, of mixed black and Amerindian heritage, who is 7 years old at the time of our first meeting, and that Nicole seems to take good, intelligent care of him.

When she begins her analysis with me, her father is in a pitiful state: seriously afflicted with Parkinson's disease, he refuses to take his prescription drugs. She criticizes acerbically this domestic tyrant for his childish behaviour. After a year and a half of her analysis, Nicole's father will finally die in rather abject conditions.

Then she has several dreams: "*In one*", she says, "*there's Victoire, my ex-girlfriend. She puts her arms around me, she's very much in love, and says 'It's good, we're going to have a child together.' But I answer, 'You didn't want one when I wanted one, now I refuse.' This is pure revenge, because in fact I really want a child.*" Nicole grasps that her disappointment in her father has been displaced onto the character of Victoire.

She talks about her last girlfriend, who has gone back overseas, and who is now with "*a pretty good man, nice, not macho, who's also really great with her child. . . . She still gives me the impression that she has a kind of emptiness inside her, that she's pretty worthless.*"

I tell that I'm struck by the way she equates femininity with emptiness and worthlessness.

Then she cries out pathetically, "*Yes, but it's terrible. I wonder: are we condemned to a form of immobility, or can we move? Can psychoanalysis change me, or only make me accept, resign myself? . . . I wonder why I've been choosing girls like that for so many years, empty, with no plans. Of course, they cling to me; that gives me control, domination. But now, I would like someone who* has *something!*"

—"That would be quite a change", I say.

—"I think that, paradoxically, it would make me feel better about myself. But it's not the same approach."

—"Not the same approach to seduction?"

—"Yes, in fact, I'm going to have to rethink that. I think that I no longer have the innocence of a certain blindness [sic]."

But once again, Nicole will quickly cover up the breach opened by her mourning for her father: she takes concrete steps to get back together with her first girlfriend, Victoire. There is no longer any question of having sex together, but they agree to live together, as partners—and Victoire herself is in the process of adopting a South American baby.

In the months that follow (her third year of psychoanalysis), Nicole will describe for me, ever more critically, an extraordinarily *macho* Victoire, who neglects her little adopted daughter and goes off to pick up girls right and left.

So Nicole herself now becomes a sort of housewife, which makes her feel identified with her mother, struggling to contain the situation, compensating for the father's shenanigans. Still, Victoire gives her the impression of being "superior".

"*I can see clearly that it was after my father's death that I came back to her. I have the impression that she's like an improved version of him* (!). *In any case, she has fought professionally; she fought more intelligently and efficiently than he did.*"

Nicole's way of referring to efficiency seems to me to touch upon the crucial question of what kind of *ego ideal* she might have at her disposal, and her need to flesh out, within herself, this central operator bound to the effective power of the father.

"*The love of my father*", she goes on, "*enabled me to acquire qualities and means; but his failure, and then his awful attitude in the face of suffering, blocked my relationship with him, had a paralyzing effect on me.*"

"*I would like to meet a man*", she suddenly blurts out. "*It seems that there would be less rivalry, because of the differences. With a woman, it's more like being in a mirror; a man is less understandable, one can have one's secret gardens, more or less comprehensible. It's exhausting with a woman, understanding each other too much, penetrating* [sic] *each other too much. Yes, it's more tiring with someone similar; the other person wants to know everything, tries for total fusion."* (Silence)

"*But after having seen the way my father treated my mother, cheating on her, reducing her to slavery, I can't trust. I can see myself living unhappily with a man I'd always expect to betray me.* (Silence)

"*I wonder why I keep letting myself decline professionally, why I've been vegetating for ten years.*"

She tells herself that she can do better than "*fucking empty, worthless girls*"; which leads her to wonder: "*What flaw is manifesting itself in me then, which I can't see?*"

—I tell her that her compulsive choice of young women who have such an obvious flaw perhaps served to exempt her from having to *play her own flaw* in romantic relations; but she has settled for a *macho* release-pleasure for a long time, while languishing in a lack of professional fulfilment.

Then she seems able to glimpse that this disavowal of the flaw in her prevents her from receiving what she needs from another person, and that in this she picks up precisely what she deplores in her father. "*With Victoire, we are differentiating ourselves more and more from one another since we've been living together. Still, I wonder why I myself have no more sex life for the past several months. I was admired for my tough, macho side. I have the impression I've gotten a new kind of defence. . . .*"

"*It seems that in me this corresponds to a de-idealization of my father. I can see how his failure was a product of his blindness, of his inability to accept advice, or medical care. He always had the utmost contempt for my uncle, his brother. Well, I can see that this modest man is now able to pass on much more to his children, that in the end he's made rather a success of his life.*"

"*My son* [then 10 years old] *irritates me. I think he's a softy, a coward, indecisive, flighty. I think that men are weak, less lucid, more dependent. I want to shake him and yell: "Be a man!"*

—I point how paradoxical such an injunction is, in light of what she has just said about men in general.

—"*Okay, I mean: be a* real *one! I'm fed up with all this bluster and pretending. I'm still hold out hope that a man could be different, to meet one . . . well, kind of like my uncle.*"

—I stress that here she seems to touch upon something important, something she cares about, when she talks about *pretending to have.*

—"*I would like to meet a concrete example of a man who's not a coward, who shows me that I'm right to hope for that. I would like to make my son into a courageous man. I don't know if this is a problem of castration....*"

—"It would be strange", I say, "if your son were the only person like that in your life."

—"*No, of course not: my brother showed courage in the end: he was able to resist my father and leave. I would need a concrete encounter with a man.*"

At this stage of the analysis, I decide to refrain from interpreting the implication in the transference of her idea of meeting *a-man–a-real-one,* because I have the impression then of a process that is both positive and *nascent:* the beginnings of a motion of desire towards a male who takes into account castration, and from whom she can therefore receive something.

One year later, as she is starting her fourth year of analysis, Nicole talks to me about writing a book on Polynesia. But she who is always so headstrong and determined is now dragging her feet when it comes to making useful contacts.... She finally recognizes: "*Yes, I am panicking about this precisely because this time it won't be bluster! The idea of getting criticized by specialists makes me completely anxious.... In retrospect, I laugh when I reread papers I wrote with such conviction a few years ago: it was the work of an amateur.... I tell myself that if I manage to make such a book, it would be the end of my analysis. It would be a real birthing, it would fulfil me.*"

—"Well, your anxiety is more understandable!" I say.

—She laughs. "*But I have the feeling it could work. My father's horrible end mustn't leave me hamstrung indefinitely. I could go to Polynesia for a few weeks; luckily I will be going to the shore then on a class trip.*"

—"But what about your analysis?"[3]

—"*The benefit of analysis is just that: being able to achieve something like that. If I give up my project because of the analysis, that would be a sign it's not working, that I'm closing myself up. For me, this is giving birth, after a wished-for pregnancy. As for my son, I also owe a debt of gratitude to his biological parents, because they made him very well.*"[4]

Through her writing project, Nicole can effectively approach the issue of *debt*. First of all with regard to the sources she has to use for her book; but also with regard to the inheritance she received from her father and the right way to use it. This makes her realize that one factor in her father's bankruptcy was his inability to refuse anything to his staff; he thought he had to act *"inexhaustible"*.

A little later she tells me a dream about fellatio: "*It's very precise, I'm performing fellatio on men that I can't see clearly, I only see their erect penis.*" She associates in two intertwined registers: on the one hand, she sees herself devoted to giving an orgasm to a male (father?) who has a penis; and on the other hand, she sees herself sucking avidly, *pumping,* she says, this same (inexhaustible?) penis. This brings back the memory of a dream where she saw herself pregnant. "*Wow!*" she shouts. "*That's the first time!*"

"*It must have to do with my book project, which I've been talking so much to you about. . . . It would be like a kind of incorporated potency. I have ancestors who played a part in the discovery of the overseas colonies. I'm probably trying to prolong some part of their adventure with my book.*"

It would be, she says again, like "*the end of an initiatory course*"—a course in which the adoption of her son may have been another important step.

But now she starts to express her satisfaction at discovering another way of being, "*using my interior*" she says, regarding her flat, where she has recently received and displayed the works of an artist friend of hers. "*I feel very good about receiving these things into my house, and at the same time receiving people who can appreciate them. Why didn't I think sooner of offering my space this way?*" She's feeling more creative now "*more receptive and fertile*". Then she starts to complain again about her *alter ego,* Victoire the swinger.

Nicole's analysis seems to bear witness to a mutative process in the patient's psychic relation with the reference of the phallus, which tends to take on for her the functionality of an authentic *signifier* in the sense that it is precisely *the possibility of its physical absence* that she comes to grasp as something that can be fertile. At the same time, we see that she is able to develop a new aptitude for entering in play in a receptive–passive mode, with a subjective enjoyment that is considerably enriched and a source of creativity.

In "Some Psychical Consequences of the Anatomical Distinction between Sexes" (1925j), Freud begins by speaking again of the little boy's usual disavowal (of the absence of the penis in the woman), and he then goes on to say: "A little girl behaves differently. She makes her judgment and her decision in a flash. She has seen it and knows that she is without it and wants to have it" (p. 252). A woman is thus characterized by the problem of obtaining the penis (of the father)—hence by a propensity towards envy of this penis in the other. But Freud adds that there are women in whom "the hope of some day obtaining a penis in spite of everything and so of becoming like a man may persist to an incredibly late age and may become a motive for strange and otherwise unaccountable actions".

We see how this second *having* of which the disavowal (of absence) consists is fundamentally different from the first (*she knows that she is without it and wants to have it*), for it stems from the idea of being constitutionally possessed of a penis. The remove between possessing by oneself (constitutionally, from birth) and receiving from another (signifier of the gift) is obviously of capital importance, to such an extent that it is precisely at this point in his work that Freud will employ for the first time the substantive form of the term *disavowal* [*Verleugnung*] which thus finally rises (1925j) to the rank of a major concept in his theory—precisely when speaking of women.

The woman who disavows (her lack of a penis) remains anchored in the idea of phallic superiority by constitution, and not received as a gift—in other words, she situates herself on the "masculine" side of sexual difference. While women who are referred to as *feminine* like to maintain more or less discreetly, among themselves, an amused consensus about the fact that no manifestly phallus-bearing person is without faults, this feminine consensus is typically missing in the lesbian. So we can consider that Nicole could progress towards being-a-woman when she hits upon the idea of meeting a man who would not be an impostor (pretending to be constitutionally phallic), but who could own up to his castration—perhaps in the same sense that Diogenes was looking for *an honest man*.

Nicole's analysis will also show her emerging from her (sexual) *latency*: during her last year of analysis, she will be able to enter into a new romantic relationship. Of course the partner is once again a woman; but this new relationship seems to have lost the "perverse" characteristics of her earlier affairs. These affairs were clearly polarized into a univocal, and somewhat fetishistic, mode of satisfaction—first with Victoire, in the position of dominated, submissive initiate, and then with later partners in a dominating, phallic mode.

It is significant that her new partner started out as a collaborator in an equal exchange in the production of Nicole's book (the appreciable success of which gave her a new lease on life). In the same sense, I will be struck to hear that Nicole—rather like Vera (chapter 2)—has finally managed to establish a new mode of interaction with her mother, involving a much richer mode of positional reversibility, and this within an exchange that is substantial, and not only fantasized.

To conclude about the key role of the qualitative mutation of the phallus as mental representation, it is as if this mutation were emblematic of the crest along which psychoanalysis is destined to *surf*: that thin line between the representation of the partial object as such, with its narcissistic freight of the organ's image, and the necessity that this same thing-representation develop a signifying potential capable of fertilizing the figures of *lack* and of the *gift*. I will say, in sum, that our *thing-representations* have the mission of coming to work as *signifiers* (as they do normally in the dream). In this respect, it seems to me that any analytic practice that lets itself stray too much to one side or the other (towards the object relation in the session, for example, the here-and-now, or towards the pure play of the verbal signifier) quickly exposes itself to a form of conceptual sterility.[5]

Now we must examine, in the next chapter, the particular vicissitude (accomplishing destiny) of the drives that is *sublimation*. First, because it contributes very much to the development of a capacity for subjective enjoyment; and also, because it enables us to better discern the very problematic nature of the (obscure) object of drive; and, finally, because it can shed light on the necessary role of the so-called *death drive* (that of unbinding) in the very process of subjectivation.

Notes

This chapter essentially returns to material presented in a conference given at the Société Psychoanalytique de Paris, May 19, 1998.

1. See the term "Phallus" in *The International Dictionary of Psychoanalysis* (de Mijolla, 2005).
2. This is probably the typical form taken by the "paternal metaphor" in the lesbian—that is, the transference onto the father of a disappointment first experienced with the mother.
3. I said this to highlight my own position of having to submit to her project.
4. This sort of grateful recognition is often lacking in pathogenic adoptive parents (see the case of Angel, in chapter 6).
5. If we may consider *ego psychology* as reductive of Freud's thinking, a certain kind of Lacanianism turning upon the verbal signifier alone would appear to be just as reductive of Lacan's thinking.

CHAPTER EIGHT

Sublimation, latency, and subjectivation

Growth at puberty is preceded by what psychoanalysts, following Freud's lead, still refer to as a *latency period*, supposed to extend from around 7 to 11 years of age. This notion of "putting into latency" is mainly intended to designate a state wherein the direct modes of drive satisfaction—that is, modes of release (pleasure)—are temporarily renounced. Freud, regarding the development of the psychic apparatus from a *genetic* perspective, situated this latency period between two "hot" periods: the so-called oedipal period, around 4 to 5 years, and the awakening of puberty—periods when the quest for satisfaction-release, notably through masturbation, tends to be heightened. Interestingly, the intermediary period called *latency* usually proves to be a decisive time for the acquisition of capacities to sublimation. This conjunction between latency and sublimation is not surprising if we consider, as Freud did, that sublimation is precisely a way of achieving drive satisfaction without release. We shall return to this idea.

In addition to my long-term clinical work with adolescents, I have had in my practice of adult treatments the opportunity to observe the particular importance of a certain latency in psychoanalysis involving *homosexual* patients, both men and women. This seems to corroborate the fact that the process of transference must often start with a moment in life when a transforming process was arrested (in these cases, probably during pre-adolescence). One can see how the treatment of Nicole (chapter 7) leads to an increased ability in her to sustain the tension of desire as well as a certain *passivation*, especially through new drive destinies of a sublimatory kind; but it took a long time for this mutation to occur, by means of a *putting into latency*[1] of her sexual activity.

It is also after latency that the crisis of puberty manifestly begins, producing something in the organism that I propose to designate as a *change of drive regime*. Here, indeed, the concept of drive—invented by Freud to designate the dynamic within the human being that serves as an intermediary between the energies of the body and the energies of the psyche—seems to describe what happens when a young person has to integrate a new (and sexual) energy, in order to become a "new subject" (Freud, 1915c). From this perspective, our work with adolescents in crisis leads us to evaluate, in every case, the extent to which the investments of the latency period have been able to *stay the course*, to adapt themselves, rather than get blasted away by the rising sexual heat of puberty.

I would say more precisely that through the torment of the change of economical regime[2] that characterizes the passage through puberty, we will observe after the fact the extent to which the putting into latency of latter childhood has permitted true (drive) sublimations to be established. Or we may find that we are dealing less with true sublimation than with defensive "reaction-formations" and counter-investments of a mainly repressive nature, which come from the famous *ego force* and as such are liable to be easily swept away by the destabilization of puberty.

Now we must re-examine the "vicissitude" of the drive that is sublimation, because it does in fact contribute in a major way to providing subjects of both sexes with an increased capacity for enjoyment and libidinal accomplishment, at the same time shedding light on the difficult question of the object of the drive.

Freud never wrote the fourth part of his 1915 "metapsychology" which was to have treated—after "Instincts and Their Vicissitudes", "Repression" (1915d), and "The Unconscious" (1915e)—that other vicissitude of the drive that is Sublimation. The latter helps to better conceive of the subject as an agent of the drive, but on two conditions: first, that sublimation be clearly distinguished from the imaginary process of *idealization* (both of the object and of the ideal ego); second (and Freud could not write this in 1915), to give full weight to the fact that the drive satisfaction without release that characterizes the achievement of sublimation situates it *beyond the pleasure principle* (1920g)—and it is through this that the subject function (subject of the drive) can better be distinguished from the narcissistic-defensive functions of the ego, which serve to reduce tensions according to the logic of the pleasure principle.

The place of idealization

Concerning idealization, the clinical treatment of adolescents enables us to gauge just how much this *imaginary* mechanism is both a defensive recourse for these youngsters and a fearsome stumbling block. At this period of life more than any other, it is useful not to mix up the registers of the "ego ideal" and the "ideal ego", for their impact (efficiency) in the subjective economy is not at all the same. Discussing Daniel Lagache, Jacques Lacan carried out critical work that constitutes an essential tool for better understanding the stumbling blocks of adolescence (Lacan, 1960a, p. 543); it is astonishing to see how (undoubtedly out of fear of *anti-Lacanianism*) many colleagues who are familiar with adolescence stubbornly maintain a conceptualization that does not take into account this groundbreaking work of Lacan, which so usefully differentiates between imaginary formations and symbolic operators.

The cult of *idols*, which, as is well known, has an important place in adolescent devotions, provides a good illustration of how these narcissistic figures of the corporeal ego, idealized and projected onto an "idol", prove to be unfit for compensating functionally for the deficiency of the internal symbolic operator that is the ego ideal. Also, one can measure very concretely the degree of internal symbolic efficiency of these instances by the yardstick of *enacted violence*. On this point, beyond the problems of adolescence, it is in fact the history of the human race as a whole that has shown us all too often how the worst outbursts of destructiveness have been engendered precisely by the worship of figures of the narcissistic ideal—Freud's *Group Psychology* (1921c) and his *Civilization and Its Discontents* (1930a [1929]) have provided incisive analyses of this phenomenon.

Already in "On Narcissism: An Introduction" (1914c), Freud categorically posited that "Idealization is a process that concerns the object; by it, that object, without any alteration in its nature, is aggrandized and exalted in the subject's mind (p. 94)". He goes on to say: "Sublimation is a process that concerns object-libido. . . . In so far as sublimation describes something that has to do with the instinct [drive] and idealization something to do with the object, the two concepts are to be distinguished from each other." And he concludes: "The formation of the ideal increases, as we have seen, the demands of the ego, and it is what acts most strongly in favour of repression; sublimation represents the issue that allows these demands to be satisfied without bringing on repression" (p. 99).

Here we must consider what Freud calls *sexual drives that have been inhibited in their aim*—that is, in their mode of being satisfied. He clearly posits that satisfaction can effectively be attained in this case but by other means than release (unloading); so repression does not have an essential role here. This is crucial to a better understanding of the specific characteristics of the sublimatory "solution".

One often observes that subjectivation gains by building itself up to sublimatory fulfilment, where the subject's enjoyment maintains a paradoxical relationship with "normal" satisfaction (through the pleasure of release/unloading), which would mark the limit of interruption, the finiteness of the *enjoyment-in-tension* of the subject (Laznik-Penot, 1990). But this kind of enjoyment, insofar as it is highly subjectivated and without release, may appear to connote a certain masochism—as if it were a way of *suffering* and *enjoying* at the same time. Benno Rosenberg (1991) rightly pointed out the key role of masochism in the very process of subjective development.

The sublimatory solution

Lacan energetically pursued Freud's arguments about the specific traits of drive sublimation, starting with Freud's premise that it is a direct and effective way of satisfying the drive. It is above all in this way that the sublimatory process is different from the compromises resulting from repression of drive representatives, with the inevitable *return of the repressed* constitutive of neurotic symptoms. If sublimation consists of a change of aim (i.e., of the mode of satisfaction) of drive activity as such, it is a path towards subjective realization that it is obviously very important for a youngster to discover and experiment as soon as possible.

In our practice we observe that what will most stimulate the child towards the discovery of sublimatory fulfilment is not principally the repression of his/her sexuality by the parent, but chiefly his/her own experience of the limited and disappointing character of the immature sexual pleasure within reach—in comparison with other things in life that he/she can already accomplish satisfactorily. From here on, it is usual to note that the inciting example of the loved adult proves to be a more decisive factor than constraints and threats—one more illustration that the "do as I say, not as I do" coming from the parent has never been very effective. . . .

Here we should better define the difference between repressive parental *superego* and the *ego ideal* that has been transmitted. I would say that the latter represents something like a *"savoir jouir"* (knowing how to enjoy) of drive activity that the youngster can perceive as being accessible to him/her, as well as recommended and appreciated. A formulation made by René Diatkine in our work with psychodrama in the early 1970s helped me to conceptualize this better: he would speak of "identifying oneself with a function" when a young person became able to manage effectively some aspect of reality (his/her enjoyment, therefore) (Diatkine, 1995). Such a formulation starts us on the way to understanding how the ego ideal is specifically constituted by the *introjection* of psychic parental *operators*, starting with the perception (no doubt a very early one) of clues to the parents' effective enjoyment, which results from a certain "know-how" with regard to reality.

This incitement by way of example (and identification) must

not be confused with the essentially threatening, intimidating, and repressive character of the superego. I suggest that the latter be characterized as the internalized signal of the limit of parental love (tolerance). We know that the threat of losing love plays a decisive role at the beginning of the process of repression (Freud placed much emphasis on this) and thus in the formation of symptoms. Its effects can be verified *a contrario* in the virulence that the superego of delinquents can show—contrary to received ideas.

Thus the treatment of adolescents in crisis obliges us to acknowledge that it is not in taking inspiration mainly from the repressive superego that we can best foster a youngster's ability to accede to sublimatory enjoyments.[3] Rather, experience leads us to believe that it is now necessary to overcome the condensation maintained by Freud with his notion of *paternal superego,* and to work at better defining the three "superegoical" instances with their complementary functions—while remarking that the field of action of each one begins where the limits of the others' efficaciousness may be felt.

Specifying the ego ideal

At the Congrès des Psychanalystes de Langue Française in Montréal, in June 2000, Jacques Mauger and Lise Monette stressed the "conceptual difficulties" that continue to stem from these three instances "so that each of them has trouble making understood what it is trying to delimit, and even more so when one tries to define them as autonomous entities, *without the dialectic that constitutes them*" (italics added).

In his report to the same congress, Gilbert Diatkine (2000) situates the superego and the ego ideal within a certain functional antagonism. Using revealing clinical illustrations drawn from his work with children, Diatkine shows how one can serve as an antidote to the other. However, he is much less clear as to the register proper to the third culprit, the "ideal ego".

I suggest that we consider that this triad (superego—ego ideal—ideal ego) can take on its tri-dimensional span and its full theoretical and practical functionality only if we stop trying to characterize the ego ideal as "ideal" in the narcissistic sense (which tends to push it back onto the ideal ego). I think it would be more fruitful to define the ego ideal as a *symbolic operator,* which as such maintains a lateral relationship (of dynamic and dialectic contiguity) with the projected narcissistic figures of the ideal ego. From this perspective, the ego ideal may be conceived of as an instance founded precisely on *introjection,* starting with the earliest relations of one life, of certain qualities perceptible in the responses of the first parental partner—and which should begin to be registered psychically as soon as the first drive exchanges have been established.

This leads me to make a second proposal, in the form of a wish: that we give up once and for all our attempts to represent the relationship of these three instances as a *genetic hierarchy*—wherein the ideal ego, for example, is envisioned as "archaic" in relation to the ego ideal, the latter being supposedly more "evolved".[4] It seems to me that this kind of developmental vision is meant to compensate for a conceptual difficulty, that of defining the respective psychic registers (imaginary, symbolic) to which these instances basically belong. The problem is that when we inflate the "genetic" point of view this way, according to a developmental linearity, we lose the dynamism of the properly *metaphorical* vision Freud introduced, which envisions a dialectical relation between synchronous heterogeneous instances.[5]

The dynamic relation between narcissistic defences and progress in subjectivation must develop itself throughout one's life. I think it is important to consider that the three registers of these instances—including the narcissistic ideal ego—continue to play a useful role, however "evolved" one may suppose oneself to be in one's development as a human subject (doesn't the configuration of our dreams constantly remind us of this?) The representative supports for narcissistic idealization must necessarily play their part in their specific register in each of us—as may often be observed in artwork. Moreover, there is nothing to suggest that each of the three ideal instances is not present in the normal child as a very early specific "core".

This said, one must also insist on the fact that sublimatory solutions prove especially well suited to integrating the disassociative component of the drive, the so-called *death drive,* in people whose love life is difficult to experience without destructive effects. Sublimations are precisely libidinal fulfilment with a particular capacity for integrating economically such a destructive dimension, notably that which comes from the earliest family experiences. Still, the sublimatory development under the aegis of the ego ideal must take place within a sufficient relation (binding) with the two other instances—superego and ideal ego.

The object of the sublimatory quest

We have already emphasized that the sublimatory mode of satisfaction is paradoxical in that it is carried out through other routes than the "normal" aim of a sexual release/unloading of drives. A question then arises: can one therefore argue that satisfaction through sublimation is not *sexual*? Freud sometimes seems not to be opposed to such a conception, and a number of other authors have been seduced by the "good news" of a libido that, though sexual in origin, would in the end become *de-sexualized*. (Phew!)

The vision, promoted by Melanie Klein (1946), of a *reparative* (and thus imaginary) goal for sublimatory activity also appears questionable. However, she should be credited with pointing out that when the subject moves to sublimate, he is pursuing something on the order of a primary-object-forever-lost. Thus the sublimatory solution appears to spring from an utterly archaic relation at the start, in one sense confirming what Freud articulated about the necessity, at the outset, for the drive activity to depend upon the object of need.

Lacan tried to show better how what he calls the *object* (*a*) targeted by the drive movement must, in a way, have been "detached" from the primordial parent–other, and this within the very operation by which the child manages to take the symbolic measure of this (maternal) partner—a notion that is somewhat convergent with the famous *depressive position* of Melanie Klein (1946). The partial objects that are psychically "detachable" in this way would thus represent something like *an obscure residue* (without mental image) of the process of symbolization of the parental partners in the earliest drive exchanges.

The original corporeality of the primary objects of the drive's quest will lead them to "fall" into the status of unconscious traces, which will tend to give rise to always approximate forms of representation. One could speak of *original repression* here; but it is probably useful to observe that these "obscure objects of desire" intrinsically belong to the psychic category of *the real*, insofar as they are the inevitable residue of the very process of symbolization (of the mother, in the first place). Indeed, this fundamental quality lets them escape the imaginary, structuring phenomenon of the mirror: as *"unspecularizable" objects* they cannot serve in the imaginary structuring of the ego, but can only cause desire in an obscure way. Lacan offered a list of such *objects a* containing not only the *organs* of the primary mother, but also her gaze, her voice, her grasp. . . .

Nevertheless, the production of such *objects-cause* (Laplanche, 1989) plays an essential role in the basis of unconscious fantasy, to the extent that, in said fantasy, the *re-presentation of the thing* staged—set into a scene—in an interactive relationship with the subject will only ever be able to represent more or less approximately (metaphorically) the real of the lost–missing object detached from the mother at the origin. This remove is exactly what sublimatory satisfaction can give us a better idea of. This is what led Lacan (1959–60) to propose a surprising definition for sublimation, as what *"raises the object to the dignity of the Thing"*!

Of course, the (partial) object that supports the activity of sublimation is generally inseparable from imaginary elaborations that have a recognized cultural value, often not very utilitarian but giving effective access to enjoyment. But Lacan insists on the *baiting* function of these artistic ornaments in comparison with what acts in a more fundamental way for the subject's enjoyment and which concerns his relation with a primordial object, called *das Ding* by Freud—the Thing, the quest for which the drive pursues. . . .

Here we should recall the problem of usage of the term "object" in psychoanalysis since it also serves to designate the partner invested in the love–hate relationship, the *counterpart other*, which is not, of course, the object of the drive but which only serves as a habitation for it, so to speak—where it can be embodied and personified. In the second part of "Instincts and Their Vicissitudes" (1915c), Freud will insist that, in his opinion, the love–hate couple essentially comes from a libidinal investment of the narcissistic register, involving the overall body image and, as such, rather removed from the basic problematic of drive.

These considerations also allow us to grasp better the essence of the process that is *art*, in that art accomplishes the sublimatory approach to something that it works to clothe imaginarily in the qualities of manifest representation of the work produced. This arises from the fact that, in psychic life, every *thing-representation* is already in itself a metaphorical re-presentation of the thing secretly at stake.

This is what the *surrealist* movement succeeded in making manifest—with the striking pertinence of Magritte's famous "*Ceci n'est pas une pipe!*" Moreover, Lacan (himself an active sympathizer of the surrealist movement in the 1930s) referred to Freud's presentation of his concept of drive (with its impulse, its aim, its object, and its source) as a "*surrealist montage*". . . .

We have already observed (chapter 1) how Freud, when trying to give an account of basic drive activity, could not avoid employing terms borrowed from medical discourse about *perversions*. So it is not surprising that we run into the same difficulty when speaking of sublimatory activity: it must indeed be remarked that in many ways sublimation maintains contiguous and intimate relations with the perverse approach.

This is no doubt due to the fact that, despite its cultural adornments, the activity of sublimation tends to place the subject (agent of the drive) in a raw relationship with *the thing* that causes its quest. It seems that the forms of art called "modern art" show this most clearly: the tendency of contemporary plastic-art forms is to neglect the imaginary adornments and trappings that were required of Classicism, in order to make perceivable a sort *brute* relation between the subject and its thing.

But it is necessary, nevertheless, to put the novelty of this phenomenon of modern art into perspective. It is striking, for example, to note in twelfth-century "courtly" literature the stunningly scabrous—and even scatological—aspects of the *troubadour repertoire* (evoked by Lacan in his *Seminar VII*: 1959–60). One could also point to the way in which certain supposedly pious frescoes of the Italian Renaissance are focused on close-ups of disconcertingly prominent posteriors, and so on.

Delinquent drive activity

Clinical experience with what are generally referred to as *psychopathic behaviours* can help to shed light on the issue of the drive's obscure object. We are seeing more and more children and adolescents who are destructive and even dangerous, and who appear to have surrendered themselves to irrepressible drive activity. The efforts of our governments to adapt to the increasing pathology of minors are well known. I would suggest that the "object" after which these repeated "actings" are desperately seeking could well be the *grasp*, the *gaze*, the *listening* of the parental other (which was deficient)—in any case, these are more likely than the manifest, ridiculously contingent objects of the cruelty of such youths. The fact that they compulsively reproduce their criminal acts as soon as the adult in charge ceases to look at them or take care of them would seem to support this view. Also supporting this view is the role of the prison as the setting sought out by some adult criminals (Claude Balier, 2002).

The constitution of subjective fantasy will still depend on the way that the primary (parental) other was able to undergo the operation of symbolization carried out by the child: a test of *mutual passivation*, through the reiterated experience of drive interaction. I have already emphasized (with reference to the case of Angel, in chapter 6) the propensity of some parents' narcissistic wounds to provoke a kind of defence that can become a lasting obstacle to their son's or daughter's work of subjectivation.

It seems that many extreme adolescent behaviours constitute a desperate attempt to overcome some deficiency in the *discourse of the media* (*Other*), broadcast everywhere in a cowardly, obliging (and commercial) way, without ever really owning up to its ethical implications, which many parents seem unable to explain to their children. So these adults can vaguely perceive the behaviour pathologies of the adolescent generation as a sort of interpretative return—savage and raw—of their own unacknowledged tendencies.

We can see how clinical work on *adolescence* can help answer the questions we have about some *bad subjects of the act* (see the case of Sophie, chapter 4), but also about those who start on the road to sublimatory activity. This calls to mind, for example, the importance, for many of today's youngsters, of participating in a creative way in making music or putting on a play—for some of them, such possibilities for sublimatory achievement may offer a chance to salvage their endangered psychic economy.[6]

Obviously this idea is the driving force behind many professionals who work in *open settings*, trying to have an effect on the future of at-risk youngsters. Through their work, they try to open as much as possible the access to constructive, creative drive satisfaction, instead of the destructive effects of pure release/unload or addictive co-excitation. Access to the solutions offered by sublimation does prove to be a decisive factor in enabling some youngsters to move beyond a dangerous situation, filled with a potential for hurt more or less clearly rooted in their family milieu. I now offer an illustration of this, with the case of an adolescent girl at serious risk whom I treated in our day hospital.

The case of Anna

The case of this teenage girl, whom I will call "Anna", shows what a decisive effect capacities for sublimation can have on the evolution of adolescents in grave difficulty. I first received Anna in our day hospital when she was 13; she came because she had been unable to attend any school. As soon as she would enter a school, she would experience dizziness and fainting spells, which left her no alternative but to beat a hasty retreat—in other words, as in any case of *school phobia*, to bolt back to her home. The fact that her symptoms seemed more hysterical-phobic than psychotic was not reassuring, since no counter-phobic strategy could enable her to overcome her terrible handicap, and this had been going on for two years—a period that corresponded, of course, with her passage through puberty.

We find out about the pathology of her immediate family as soon as we meet her father, who is himself completely *delusive* in an active and persecutory mode. A cultured but marginalized man, he had been a lawyer, before finally being disbarred. The disastrous consequences on the family of this man's paranoid delusions have been attenuated in part by his intellect and his sense of humour. But the damage has worsened from year to year: practically excluded from any professional activity, the father proves to be incapable of negotiating any kind of tolerable relationship in domestic life, especially with his parents-in-law, whom he accuses of "trading in souls", as well as in organs. . . .

Anna's mother is a submissive wife through thick and thin, and she is obviously smitten with her husband. Through her husband's delusions she is undoubtedly settling some rather serious scores with her own parents, who, she says, did not love her. Financially, the mother's parents have the upper hand, which gives them a say in the children's upbringing—especially given the professional failure of Anna's father, who, despite his prestigious law-school degrees, is now reduced to indigence and the consolations of red wine. But nothing seems to chip away at his domestic powers: he literally reigns over his subjugated wife and his four daughters.

Anna is the second child and enjoys a privileged relationship with her father, who often says he recognizes himself most of all in this intellectual, headstrong daughter. As for the eldest daughter, she seems to have decided to follow the example of the maternal grandfather in choosing to study chemistry. The two youngest ones, who are twins, are clearly suffering, especially in their adaptation to the beginning of elementary school.

During the two years following Anna's admission, we manage to maintain a kind of amicable balance, receiving the parents according to our usual protocol of monthly meetings, including the *referent* caregivers and the regular—and colourful—participation of Anna's father. All of us who work with Anna have stoically decided not to provoke a rupture with the delusive aspect of her father's speech—and not to make him *lose face* (we know that the social services had already been alerted by the primary school attended by the twins). Anna's mother constantly adopts an ambiguous attitude towards her husband's delusive discourse: she just smiles or discreetly rolls her eyes, indicating nonetheless *minimal* derision of her sovereign spouse, without going so far as to disavow him in practice.

So for two years, Anna benefited rather well from activities in the day hospital, especially the courses and pedagogical groups, where her participation was of the highest quality. Her personal creativity earned her the appreciation of everyone. She was soon ready to pass her junior high school examinations (O levels). But the team was worried on account of her extreme thinness and anorexic tendencies. Along the same hysterical–anorexic lines, there was her behaviour towards her peers: apparently sociable and open, but still rather distanced, lacking in affective involvement. Thus she would participate, with a certain authority, in the romantic relations of her friends, but always at a certain remove, as a rather inventive *third party* (a little like a *duenna*, or a *go-between*).

With her austere, willowy physique and her zeal for minding other people's business, she reminded me of that tireless social activist who became Freud's first patient, Bertha Pappenheim, alias Anna O. Our Anna will resemble Freud's patient to the point of experiencing a *nervous pregnancy*—at the age of 15—after having "dated" a boy for the first time. She will keep it secret for several months before "spilling" the matter to our nurse.

However, the father's presence continues to weigh on the household; he never leaves the house now, having no more work outside it. He demands that his daughters be continually present, thus cutting them off from any social life. He obliges them to stay at the dinner table for hours, listening to his delusive (and increasingly drunken) monologues. We feel that the moment of confrontation cannot be put off much longer. We are more and more considering requesting that social services investigate this family again, but we are held back by the fear that this could break Anna's treatment. It was when we suggested a *group home* solution for Anna that the father rose with dignity, ordering his wife and daughter to leave with him. The therapeutic rupture has been accomplished. . . .

At that time, Anna was 16 and had just passed her exams with flying colours. She had also written and performed, with other adolescents in our theatre workshop, a play so passionate and murderous it makes Bizet's *Carmen* look like a nice story. . . .

Anna does not complain very much about her reclusive situation; her good grades make her optimistic about passing her baccalaureate (A levels) as an independent candidate. Her elder sister, on the other hand, has just failed her exam to enter pharmaceutical school and consequently has had to give up a recently acquired room in a university dormitory. But Anna can see a light at the end of the tunnel: she says she is certain that her father, being very attached to legality (perhaps to the point of madness), will recognize that she has reached the age of legal majority when she turns 18 soon, as he did for her elder sister.

But Anna does not pass her baccalaureate exam, a setback that, for someone so gifted, must be seen as a kind of *parapraxis*. The following autumn, once she has reached her long-awaited majority, we receive a *reminder letter* from her in which talks about falling back on a childcare certification, so that she could at least earn a little money for her family.... In this way we re-established contact with her. Still, she would later try to commit suicide with pills, and afterwards be confined to a hospital for a brief period, before being able to re-enter our day hospital, thanks to the social-security coverage of her mother (no doubt frightened by Anna's suicide attempt). This time her father did not protest. In fact, he did not appear at all. He was more and more wrapped up in his delusions, and in any case seemed to consider that his permission was no longer required.

Anna says that after she failed her baccalaureate, her father insisted on making a long declaration, expressing his satisfaction at how much "like him" this daughter was. This probably helped to send her into despair, as she was unable to bear such a narcissistic *identification,* with its explicitly destructive dimension.

She makes an intensive return to the activities of the day hospital, repeating the second form and preparing to take her baccalaureate exam again, concentrating on the humanities. At first she seems rather happy and fulfilled, very involved, though still a little "detached". But her subjective life is sorely tested by her having to survive on her own, away from her parents' home, sharing a studio apartment with her sister in exchange for hours of babysitting. She decides to arrange for individual psychotherapy with a psychoanalyst in the day hospital—convinced that she has to ready herself for her father's psychic and mental collapse and having no illusions about her mother, who is immature, even downright childish. Eventually Anna will be able to put into words and work on her feeling of inner destruction and her problems with affective exchanges.

Discussion of the case

With this brief account, I hope that I have managed to communicate the impression we had of seeing a kind of "miracle" in the girl's remarkable ability to invest in the activities of sublimation—which truly helped her to live again, despite the daily catastrophe of her family.

The central paradox of this case is that the patient shows every indication of having a rather good *paternal internal imago*! . . . Indeed it is as though Anna was able to accomplish a good introjection of efficient internal mediators—precisely because (I would argue) it happened to designate as *ego ideal*. Despite the flamboyant outbursts of a father who abused her with his incestuous demands, something will be transmitted, something on the order of an incitement to sublimatory libidinal investments, producing in this girl an ability to "treat" well with a certain number of cultural and creative tools. Anna seems to have been able to identify positively with certain of her father's capacities for achieving enjoyment through sublimation and to have given herself the tools for this—the psychic operators.

This girl certainly reminds one of some cases of the children of mentally ill parents who have had to force themselves to become mature, except that she was able to maintain a very adolescent playfulness and an almost furious creativity. Her creative abilities clearly differentiate her from *operatory* and hyper-reasonable tendencies of most so called therapist–children.

Moreover, contrary to pathologies of adolescence referred to as "behavioural", Anna has very little need to resort to substitute fillers, whether *idolizing* (ideal ego) or *addictive*, nor to violent, destructive *acts*. However, one can still worry about whether in the future she will be able to have a love life. With her predilection for boys in serious inner turmoil, Anna does not yet seem have within herself the "inner paths" (Chabert, 1999) that would allow her to have a positive experience of a loving (and sexually differentiated) partnership.

On the other hand, she demonstrates the highest degree of what Winnicott (1971a) calls "the capacity for being alone", a capacity that is obviously highly determined by one's aptitude for the activities of sublimation. In this she is the polar opposite of many more or less destructive behaviours that we have to deal with in our day hospital. The contrast lies mainly in the difference of *drive solutions* that the youngster is able to employ as an outlet for his/her existential drama. It will also be necessary for these solutions to integrate the dis-associative component of the drive, called the *death drive*—as is precisely true of sublimation activities.

Let us try to go further into the fundamental lesson that the sublimatory mode of drive satisfaction has to teach us as a subjective solution. We have seen that in Lacan's theoretical construction, the obscure *thing*—around which the drive's trajectory gravitates—holds an essential place, one that is tenaciously ignored in non-Lacanian circles. The theoretical object that Lacan calls *little a* does play for him a role that is just as decisive as that of the signifier—for the good reason that it is an inevitable corollary of the signifier, since the proper of every act of symbolization and every signifying act in the human being would be to produce a residue of the *real* in the psyche.

It is in the child's effort to better discern, symbolically, his/her primordial partner that something—of the gaze, of the voice, of the grasp, and so forth—will be "detached",[7] or would "fall off" this "other" (once recognized as such), and thenceforth come to constitute a register of unconscious internal objects, irreducibly resistant to the symbolic register, since they cannot be represented as such, and even to the imaginary register, since they cannot be *specularized* (imaginarily represented)

We can see that *signifier* and *object a* constitute the two fundamental tools of Lacanian theory. One may also note that the inevitable production of a residue of the *real* within every signifying activity is, in a certain way, analogous with what Freud (1930a [1929]) says about sublimation: that the drive cannot be wholly satisfied by it—that there will always be *something left over*.

The necessary role of the so-called death drive

Let us now return to the functional duality of *ego/subject* that this book proposes to clarify. Regarding sublimation, we have said that such a differentiation can only take on its full metapsychological conceptualization if we take into account the turning point in Freud's thinking, what René Roussillon (1995) calls "the second metapsychology", involving the "beyond the pleasure principle" (Freud, 1920g). Because of the very fact that the subject appears through the passivation of the drive activity, it belongs to this *beyond*; and it is in this that we can better distinguish, within the equivocal Freudian *Ich*, what belongs to the subject function from what devolves to the ego. It is in this sense that Lacan suggests the subject be conceived of as *"beyond the ego"*—that is, beyond the pleasure principle—unlike the identifications that make up the ego and that are in the service of the pleasure principle.

Now whoever attempts any creative act—writing, for example—can experience the impermanent, uncertain, and even baffling character of the subject of inspiration. We have heard of artists wake up every morning anxious that they may have lost the inner subject of yesterday's creative movement (it would be easy to draw an analogy with one's sexual inspiration).

But the energetic impulse that constitutes the *id of the drive* must, if it is to take shape, cut a path through the apparatus of the ego; this is indispensable to making of him/herself an imaginary representation. So the subject of the drive can acquire *formal* representation (in fantasy in particular), and thus imaginary substance, only though the ego—with the inevitable *alienation* that this entails in the contingencies of body image and successive identificatory supports.

In addition, the fact that true subjectivation starts specifically with the (passive-masochistic) reversal of drive satisfaction tends to inscribe the process of subjectivation itself within the *economical paradox* that Freud questioned so much, especially starting from masochism (1924c), which he realized that the pleasure principle alone could not account for. This led him to give a new form to the duality, posing as one of his terms what he calls (perhaps improperly)[8] the *death drive* (it is, rather, a *dissociation drive*), which he will henceforth place in dynamic opposition to *Eros*, the principle of libidinal binding.

Psychoanalysts, who are mainly concerned with the ego as an agent of integration and control, do not seem inclined to use the notion of the death drive. Thus Paul Denis (1997) proposes that drive be conceived as essentially having two components: one part of *control* (mastering) directed at the object, and another part, a tendency to *satisfaction*, which Denis considers as belonging to the register of a "passive" experience. This configuration seems sufficient to him to do without Freud's second theory of drive duality, and the dialectic role it attributes to the so-called death drive.

But how can we evacuate the fundamental role of *Antéros* (Braunschweig & Fain, 1971), which is inseparable from the *beyond the pleasure principle*? Is this not indispensable to conceiving of the paradox of subjectivation, which implies an enjoyment in tension that cannot be explained either by the pleasure of release or by egoistic control alone? The pairing of control and satisfaction envisioned by Paul Denis as being enough to account for the life of the drives reveals itself to be unable (among other things) to show specifically what characterizes the sublimatory fate and makes it eminently able to subjectivate.

On good parental investment

Here we touch upon a question that is obviously of primary importance in the genesis of mental disorders: what are the characteristics of "good" parental investment? Indeed, it is hard to say exactly what makes such investment *"good enough"* (Winnicott, 1971a)—in terms of projected narcissistic libido, in terms of control-satisfaction, or in terms of release-satisfaction—or, for that matter, in terms of any combination of the above, in any proportions. We know enough about the alienating effects that each of these three modes of investment can have upon a child, however they are mixed together.

This is why I would suggest that a decisive component of this "good enough" is precisely its *sublimated* quality. It must be an investment animated by effective drive satisfaction—not reactional formation, and not "false self"—an investment that does not seek incestuous release, so *degrading* for the child thus used, and is also distinct from the satisfaction of control and narcissistic (*alienating*) confusion.

We can see, then, that a certain parental *detachment* is necessary to ensure sufficient respect for the subject that is supposed to be on its way, and that this implies letting a component of *unbinding* play in the investment, in order to invite the child (by anticipation) to *ex-sist* as a subject. The investment's component of sublimatory detachment helps the parent to lend him/herself to certain *passivation* in the drive exchanges with the child—an essential attitude if the parent is to receive well the child's drive initiatives and respond in a way that fosters subjectivation. There must also be a certain detachment in the primary parent to allow a *third person* to be introduced to the child, onto whom certain qualities of the original maternal investment will be displaced. This is what is supposed to be placed onto the father—a necessary transference or "metaphor",[9] indispensable as such in enabling the deployment of the play of psychic representations.

Concerning the necessary role of the *unbinding drive* in subjectivation, Jean Laplanche (1998) has advanced an idea that could animate a fundamental debate. He situates the life drive, *Eros*, more on the side of *narcissism*—since, as he notes, it has a fundamental tendency to "*make of the one*"—while considering the death drive as an element of the sexual drive activity. From this perspective, he invites us to imagine how a "pure culture" of Eros-binding would render any kind of otherness impossible—along with any kind of erotic life.

As excess of binding is opposed to the *ex-sistence* of a subject of desire; thus the unbinding drive must necessarily play its dialectical role in the sense of *de-fusion*—what someone in a supervision group wittily termed "*untying the subject*". There is the principle of balance—in rather the way that *centrifugal* force must compensate for the force of *attraction* in order to keep bodies from imploding (and producing "white dwarves", or "black holes"). The paradox of the death drive's role also calls to mind Heraclitus' sublime formula (cited by Lacan), which puns on the Greek words *bios*, used for the archer's bow: "Its name is life (*bios*), but its job is death. . . ."

As for Lacan, he came to link this dissociation drive with the fact that the human speaks. He considers that it is specific to what he calls the "*parlêtre*" (in other words, "speak-being"), that it is inherent in the human subject. In this he differs sharply from Freud's biologizing hypotheses in *Beyond the Pleasure Principle*. He insists, rather, on the remarkably transitory character of *instinctual montages* in the human newborn. This is in agreement with the necessity—medically verifiable—that there is a sort of *relay* run through the baby's interactive experiences with the adult. If such relays are lacking, if they are not of sufficient quality, the child's development will be hampered. In the same way, we regularly observe in paediatric psychiatric treatments how certain signs of *immaturity* or *irritability* on a child's electro-encephalogram tend to become normal as the child acquires the psychic means for dealing with his excitations (through play, language, representation, . . .).

Borderline treatments

We have noted how Freud, trying to render an account of elementary drive activity, was unable to avoid using medical language about *perversions*—and this well before he was capable of explaining the death drive's necessary contribution. Now it is precisely in the treatment of what are called *borderline states* that we can best grasp the decisive importance of access to the possibility of reversing modes of satisfaction of the drive exchange: from active to passive, and vice versa, by way of the auto-erotic. We can perceive this within the interplay of the transference. It is surely not by chance that André Green (1980) came to promote the subjectivating role of drive *passivation* at the same time that his analytic practice was leading him to identify the characteristics specific to *borderline* patients.

It has become usual to designate as *borderline* those patients—more and more numerous, it seems, in our postmodern society—in whom the destructive impulse gives substance not to repression that would produce inhibitions or neurotic symptoms but, rather, to "solutions" involving action and release, or exciting addictiveness.

In the United States, Otto Kernberg (1997) has worked to specify that vast category of patients through nosographic research, with the aid of diagnostic tests. In Lyon, Jean Bergeret (1986) worked for a long time on a similar project. It seems, however, that the current tendency of French authors is to adopt a functional, rather than structural, view of this nebulous category of patients.

In this way, Jean-Jacques Rassial (1997) has recently returned to this issue, in the form of a discussion of the innovative ideas proposed by André Green. Above all, he intends to consider the borderline state as it attests to a particular relationship between these subjects and *their act*. The borderline symptom is thus envisaged by him, following Jacques Lacan's last seminars, with what the latter called "the *sinthôme*" in order to emphasize the symptom's role in repairing some defect in the psychic structure. The essential job of the symptom would thus be to "hold up" this structure, so to speak. This conception implies a mode of intervention by the psychoanalyst that differs radically from that of doctor who attacks the symptoms.

From the perspective of this symptomatology dominated by the passage to the act, the *borderline state* is often compared to the adolescent state. This is a rather optimistic way of looking at the situation, since it highlights the dimension of *immaturity* and therefore of the possibility for subjective enrichment—on condition that a certain subjectivation of the borderline symptom itself can be accomplished. Rassial (1997) is certainly right, then, to insist that the borderline state cannot be characterized by the idea that it is resistant to classical psychoanalytic treatment. On the contrary, we frequently observe that these patients respond remarkably well to analysis. I myself have frequently observed this in my supervision work: after an eventful, often stormy beginning, one is often surprised to see a patient at first judged to be *borderline* integrating the process very well. Such an evolution—which can sometimes be very quick—depends, of course, on the psychoanalyst's ability not to stint on his or her own involvement in the transference and countertransference interaction. For if the therapist is even a little *phobic*, or is determined to remain reserved in order to ensure the *asepsis* of the psychoanalytic field, his or her attitude will tend, rather, to exacerbate the (acted) *pro-vocations* of this kind of patient.

Otto Kernberg (1997) recommends interpretation as soon as possible—starting with the initial interviews—of the transference dispositions that can be discerned in the first dreams recounted by a borderline analysand, especially in the case of a *negative transference*. Indeed, Kernberg considers that this is the best way to make these patients perceive the interest of a type of *psychic binding* that can integrate their destructive dimensions (up until then dealt with by means of the passage to the act) into a dynamic fantasy life, even if its content seems decidedly *borderline*.

It seems to me that a comparison of the effectiveness of these borderline treatments with those of the more neurotic patient would not necessarily favour the latter. Often patients whose ego has a greater capacity for inhibition turn out not to be best suited to carrying out a truly transforming process, or even to developing a subjective grasp of their implication as subject—their *involvement* as an agent of the drive. . . . But the analyst who likes treatments with a little adventure quickly understands, with borderline patients, the interest of distinguishing, as I propose to do here, what is proper to the subject function from the repressive functions of the ego.

This could lead to a sort of "In Praise of the Borderline Subject", as well as of a desirable persistence of a minimum of *adolescence in the adult*. This perspective leads us to step back a little from the area of our clinical work in order to wonder if the prevalence of what we call *borderline states* in the cultural life of a given era would not bear witness (symptomatically) to the fact that the era in question is one of *mutation* for civilization.

Jean Bergeret (1986) has insisted on the *traumatic* factor at work in the genesis of the borderline state; most notably, he points out the frequency of parental figures inclined to *incestuous* abuse. But this can also indicate a destabilization of the cultural guard-rails of the era. Indeed, it is striking to see how certain *turning points* in history have favoured borderline-type personalities in politics and art. I am thinking, for example, of the critical mutation of the Greek world towards the Hellenistic mentality, with the emergence of young leaders like Alexander, Alcibiades, and many others, rather characteristic of borderline personalities. There is also the terrible end of the Middle Ages, with François Villon sounding an astonishing "modern" note in his *Ballad of the Hanged Men* in its way of treating the destructive dimension (like Baudelaire in *Les Fleurs du Mal*).

Nevertheless, a searching comparison of the effects of psychoanalysis on neurotic and borderline patients reveals what is the thorniest point in psychoanalytic practice: that the *true subject* (*subject of drive, subject of desire*) maintains close ties with the *perverse position*. Freud's detractors—and afterwards Lacan's—have made this point into their battering ram. It is around this issue that an *ethics* is still being sought today, an ethics capable of sustaining the psychoanalyst's approach, centred upon the unconscious subject of desire. Following the model of Freud's famous saying in *Studies on Hysteria* (1895d), we can continue to wonder which—neuroses or borderline states—are the functional "reverse" of the other! . . .

Freud described well the strategy proper to the neurotic who strives, in one way or another, *not to let something be done to her*! . . . Thus I think it logical, in the development of this book, to recount in the next chapter a session from the treatment of a hysterical–phobic patient; for what happens in the session seems to me a good illustration of what often goes on in the "talking cure": the analysand subject is led to be more willing *to let something be done to her/him* by the signifiers at work in her/his Unconscious. Indeed, it can happen that these signifiers will come barging into the session's discourse like intruders: stones that the (ego) builder would have liked to reject but will turn out to be the cornerstones, or even formidable levers, capable of surprising effects in freeing up the drives and developing more subjectivation.

Notes

1. With Michel de M'Uzan, we began a discussion in the Advanced Seminar in January 1998 in order to determine whether the end of an analysis was more like adolescence, or more like latency. . . .

2. In the sense, once again, that we speak of a motor-changing regime.

3. This idea tends to generate some awkward applications, like the policy of some extreme rightist municipal governments, in the Midi region of France, of systematically eliminating funding for street entertainers in order to hire more police officers.

4. My two propositions are opposed to some of Janine Chasseguet-Smirgel's (1973) ideas.

5. This is a tendency of César and Sara Botella's 2001 report, "Figurabilité et régrédience".

6. A remarkable cinematic illustration of this sort of case, it seems to me, is the character of the brilliant and sadly psychopathic guitarist played by Sean Penn in Woody Allen's 1999 film, *Sweet and Low Down*.

7. It was Freud, of course, who inaugurated this notion by conceiving,

after his own fashion, a first series of objects that could be detached from the maternal—the famous "symbolic equation", breast–faeces–penis–baby.

8. In his report to the Congrès des Psychanalystes de Langue Française of 1998, Claude Smadja speaks about the death drive in the following terms: "It is not therefore a drive to die, but a negative force which can be conceived of only in duality with the life drive. It is a positive–negative pair, as in physics."

9. Lacan developed this notion of the paternal metaphor (displacement of the primal investment), which could help to stimulate contemporary reflections.

CHAPTER NINE

Unexpected drive subjects in the session

It frequently happens during a session of psychoanalytic cure that something incongruous arises in the course of the analysand's speech, and goes on recurring in an insistent way. In the context of the imaginary relationship that had been established with that patient, such an expression will attract our attention, insofar as it seems rather *strange*, as if coming from elsewhere—from that *"other scene"* of which Freud speaks in *The Interpretation of Dreams* (1900a), the stage on which are unfurled the unconscious significations primarily linked with the drive representatives.

When a speech element of this order attracts our attention during a session, we perceive it as odd, displaced, even as we suppose it to be bearing, in some confused way, through its very insistence, a particular charge of *signification*, which it transports—rather like the "smugglers" of the Unconscious, in Freud's favourite image. And in fact, if we can only give this intruder the right to move freely about in the treatment, it will often prove to have a highly meaningful drive potential.

Here I would like to show the analyst's function in the session, which is precisely to not miss a chance to seize upon such manifestations, capable of giving rise to a "new subject". This is one reason for what we refer to as our *evenly suspended attention*. I shall try to illustrate this with a single session of a treatment.[1]

A typical session

The patient is a woman in her mid-thirties, whose neurotic ego has a predilection for using inhibiting mechanisms to give her some imaginary control over her drives. Coming from a family of modest means and Catholic convictions, living in a provincial city, she has more or less avoided until now any complete sexual relation. I will just add that she is from a big family, being one of five daughters and exactly in the middle of the birth order, with two older and two younger sisters.

The session I am going to relate occurred five years into a treatment that had been rather discouraging for me, despite the apparently good attitude of the patient. Her manifest zeal usually served to *neutralize* my interpretations and to block any opening for drive content that might appear during the sessions. My impression is that, in sum, she rendered me *powerless*, and her defence system was mobilized in a tenacious refusal of her own femininity.

She begins by saying that she feels happy to have a dream to tell me. It is her habit to write down her dreams diligently and present them to me as a "gift", but then to provide rather little in the way of associative work.

This is her dream: "*I see a little girl, who is running, running away from a house ; I perceive that she is nearly naked, and I can see that the skin of her body has a strange colour, a bright pink, especially her lower body. . . . It suggests something unhealthy, either the result of mistreatment . . . or perhaps some treatment she's fleeing?*"

She vaguely ponders these hypotheses and then prepares to move on to an account of another dream she had the same night. It is characteristic of her that she keeps herself from going much beyond the *manifest* content of her dream material; this time, I decide to stop her by saying something: "*It is the lower body that seems unhealthy to you?*" This intervention is less an interpretation than a reiteration of her own words, wherein I nevertheless try to call her attention to a possible erotic undertone.

Then she squirms a little and exclaims: "*Ah! that's it! Now I remember a word from the dream I have been looking for, a word that is hard to pronounce; that is, well, it's the word . . . thigh! . . .*" It is obviously an effort for her to utter it, and she right away associates to a scene of the day before, at her choir practice: the choirmaster (with whom, as one might expect, she wonders if she is not a little in love) has them do relaxation exercises, naming the parts of the body one by one, and this time he mentioned "*your thighs*". She remarks that this is a much "*cruder*" word than legs.

Then she returns to the dream: "*If the little girl is running away, it is not for nothing, she has good reasons. I can see a very cold woman inside the house, probably the lady of the house; it's understandable that the little girl is fleeing her.* (Silence.)

I remark then: "You were saying that the little girl was perhaps fleeing some treatment?" This is a way of highlighting what the dream conveys of *her transference* onto me, with a dimension of ambivalence that has been quite marked for some time.

She laughs: "*It's true that I was speaking, last time, about quitting the treatment! But then, it's funny: the lady of the house—would that be YOU?*" And then, addressing me in an increasingly sarcastic tone: "*Tell me, it's not a problem for you that I identify you with a woman? That I change your sex like that?*" (She chuckles.) "*Until now, I thought of you mainly as a* ferryman [*passeur*[2]], *yes, a kind of* ferryman. . . . *But here, I am now the one who is the* ferryman! *Ah, it rather pleases me to be a* ferryman."

A word repeated in this way—four times in three sentences—and with such insistence, has to intrigue me, and I decide to bring her back to it: "*passeur?*" [*ferryman?*], without myself being very aware that it could have double meaning, because *passeur* sounds like "*pas-soeur*"—that is, "non-sister". This is what most French analysts call a *signifier*—a word or an image particularly loaded with significations.

She laughs again: "*Oh, yes, that would be like a sort of false brother, or, rather, a false sister. . . .*

"*But I am going to speak in any case about the other dream, the one you prevented me from telling. It is vaguer. It is a story about a plague, damage caused by some kind of grasshopper. I can see them: they are horrible to see"* (she shivers visibly), *"a slimy kind of beast, sticking to your skin and mounting you everywhere—if you see what I mean. . . ."*

That leads her back to her first dream: *"In fact, this story of the ferryman is like a passage to Hell. That's it."* (Silence.) *"Now, what was the name of that famous ferryman of Antiquity? Ah,* Chiron! *No? Yes! That's it:* Chiron."[3]

At this point, I make my fourth intervention, formulating: "Who shits roundly?" [*chie rond*]. To which the patient reacts immediately with laughter. Then she associates to scenes from her childhood: mornings at home before leaving for school. There was only one toilet, and all the sisters had to take turns going—"*Scenes of familial defecation*", she comments.

"*And it just so happens that this morning—oh! This is difficult to say, too—at home, on the toilet, well, I noticed something. I realized I had better spread my . . . thighs, yes, to . . . shit better when I was pushing. But still, I kept them closed. You know that's a problem for me.*"

She ends the session by referring to the failure of the rare sexual experiences she had attempted with men—none of whom were able to penetrate her.

It would become clear to me, but only *afterwards*, that this particular session had a mutative effect on the progress of the treatment. It effected a kind of (re)vitalization of the patient's material, which then took on a new drive charge, within a mainly *anal thematic*. I would also point out a change in the presentation and manner of speaking of this young woman, who subsequently seemed to become more seductive. She dropped the mixture of conformist blandness and aggressiveness that, up till then, had constituted her way of defending herself against anything that could move her, stopping it short.

This reminded me of the polemic unleashed (Borch-Jacobsen, 2001) over the seminal case of the psychoanalytic adventure, the case of Bertha Pappenheim—*alias* Anna O.—with her ferocious and persistent rejection of the feminine sexual position. I thought also of Dora's disdainful words—"*Has anything so very remarkable come out?*"—just before she broke off her treatment with Freud. My patient of the 1990s also had a way of trivializing my interventions—just as she had shrunk the penises of her sexual partners.

The direct signifying route

In the session reported above, the interpretative style that I thought it best to adopt in my two last interventions essentially consisted of simply sending back to the patient two *"signifiers"* that she herself had already repeated in her discourse—*passeur* and *Chiron*.

She is then immediately able to grasp the polysemic effect. The subjective re-appropriation of her slip *Chiron* (instead of *Charon*) gives her manifest pleasure, as if she were enjoying a joke. Above all, her awareness of the *signifier* will turn out to be a key that opens up a whole area of drive (anal, in this case), with the new subjectivity that accompanies it. This effect will continue throughout future sessions.

Such an effect of drive opening appeared just after my second intervention (*You were saying that the little girl was perhaps fleeing some treatment?*), when she was surprised by the idea of the analyst's "sex change". The patient then grasped that a bad (intrusive) treatment by a mother could make a daughter thwart any future partner's attempt to get between her thighs, as it had for a long time prevented her from accepting "penetration" by her analyst's words. She was able to connect more with an eroticism that still tends to condense anus and vagina; from that moment on, we see her verbalizing this anal–vaginal confusion more in the sessions.

Wasn't it another happy inspiration on the part of the famous Amazon patient, Anna O., to have called the first steps of the talking cure *chimney sweeping*?

These excerpts from a "classical treatment" provide material for a reconsideration of what we have been saying about the *passion of the subject*. The patient in the above session (finally) showed herself capable of *letting something be done to her*: letting herself be acted upon by the sudden eruption of a representative of her repressed drive activity—in this case, two verbal *signifiers*. This illustrates a direct way of bringing the signifier and the drive subject into relation, one that nearly dispenses with the imaginary detour through corporeal, ego-to-ego representations.

The style of intervention that I have chosen to use here, which consists in simply sending back the two signifiers (*passeur* and *Chiron*) to the patient, weird in their very insistence in her speech, was probably appropriate in these circumstances. But things could have been done in a different way—for example, by emphasizing the aggressive charge manifested in her satisfaction at having made me undergo a "sex-change" or her need to dominate; or, as some colleagues (particularly Greek ones!) have ventured to suggest, by making use of the imaginary charge of the centaur Chiron. . . . Such interventions would probably have produced other effects. As a consequence of my intervention in this session, this young woman began to treat me more in the following session as if I were in the place of a drive object (stool–penis); I have learned to consider this as a rather good gauge of the accomplishment of the analytic process in a hysterical–phobic patient ruled by a strongly inhibiting and idealizing ego.

The patient's consenting to open up to the drive charge smuggled in by the signifiers she has unwittingly produced leads to the emergence in her of something like a *new drive subject:* a "bad sister" in the throes of anal rivalry, a bad *shitter* reluctant to spread her thighs to let the stool pass through, in one direction, and to let the penis pass, in the other. . . . An increased subjectivation of her anal–vaginal drive activity will thus directly result from her having been able to experience this relation of *passivation* with regard to these odd signifiers, in interaction with me.

I would afterward be struck by the new phallic efficiency demonstrated by this young woman, not only in her improved capacities for seduction, but also in her successfully undertaking new studies leading to more fruitful professional pursuits.

The "L" schema

As this work nears the end of its trajectory, it seems to me a good time to bring together what I have been saying. I will begin by presenting a topical schema providing a certain formalization of the functional distinction between drive subject and narcissistic ego. Thus I reproduce now in Figure 1 the "L" schema proposed by Lacan, starting with his seminar of 1954 (Lacan, 1954–55).[4]

This model formalizes a *topic* of the psychic apparatus constituted by two perpendicular connecting axes: on the one hand, that of the *ego* (a) in imaginary relation with the *other counterpart*

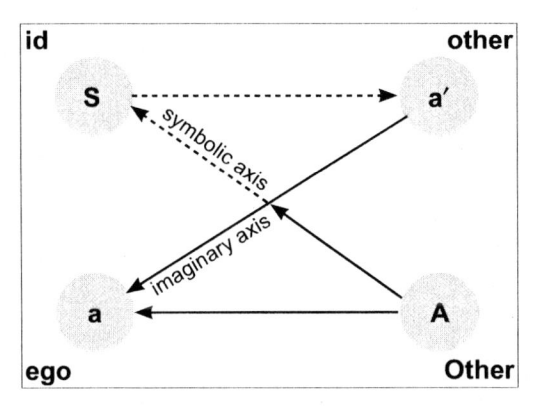

```
         id                              other
          S ←---------------------→ a′
             ˙˙˙˙symbolic axis˙˙˙
                      ╲    ╱
                   imaginary axis
                      ╱    ╲
          a ←────────────────── A
         ego                             Other
```

FIGURE 1. The L schema.

(other corporeal ego) and, on the other hand, that of the *subject* (S) in relation with the unconscious messages from *the Other*. What is remarkable here is that the subject is situated on the side of the *id*, of the Freudian *das Es* (playing, in passing, on the consonance S–Es). This is a literal illustration of Freud's well-known formula *"Wo Es war, soll Ich werden"*—where it (*id*) was, *I* must come to be.

So there is an intersection between the two directing and complementary axes of psychic life: on the one hand, the one that ties one's own-ego with the other-ego in the specular (real-imaginary) experience; and, on the other hand, that (real-symbolic) which ties the subject to the drive activity of the id through the symbolic system of exchanges. We know that Lacan designates the Other as the "place" of the reserve of signifiers that can determine the subject; thus, it is from here that will start the vector called "Unconscious" consisting of "signifying chains"—messages composed of representations of things or of words which will tend to cut through the axis of the imaginary ego–other relation, what Lacan calls the "wall of the imaginary".

Revisiting the session recounted above from this perspective, I would say that strange signifiers (like *pas-soeur*) pop up where the arrow of the Unconscious (*Ucs*) vector crosses the ego's imaginary relation with the other ego (the analyst). It is thus in the very field of the ego relation in the session that this other thing from elsewhere—this *other scene* (Freud, 1900a)—will appear and return with insistence.

Lacan constantly emphasizes that the "imaginary wall" of the ego-to-ego relation tends in practice—in daily life, of course, but also in the session if the analyst isn't careful enough—to play a role of obstructing the unconscious message that generates the subject function.

To better illustrate this, he uses the model of the *diode lamp*, within which one can see that the passage of an electric current inside a perpendicular grill can interrupt, by intercepting it, a bunch of particles circulating between anode and cathode. This is a way of giving formal representation to the antagonism between ego and (*Ucs*) subject: the imaginary ego-to-ego relation is able to intercept the subjective relationship with unconscious signifiers. In fact, this is just one possible way of representing (always metaphorically!) the topical division that constitutes the human psychic apparatus.

We have seen how what I am saying here about the *passion of the subject* springs from a rereading of Freud's model of the drive, and the revision of this by Lacan in the light of *Beyond the Pleasure Principle*. Such an approach effectively leads us to differentiate, within the Freudian *Ich*, a subject function that is in dynamic (dialectic) opposition to the defensive function of the ego. I can say that it has often been useful, in my practice as a psychoanalyst dealing with certain grave disorders of subjectivation in teenagers, to refer to this *L schema* topic.

It is perhaps not unhelpful to recall here that no psychoanalytic topic can claim to invalidate the preceding ones, nor to substitute for them, as the second topic that Freud proposed after 1920 never rendered the first one obsolete.

This said, one can understand why certain colleagues are still reluctant concerning what they see as the radicalization of a kind of *structural splitting* between drive subject and narcissistic ego, given that these two registers must necessarily and continually be woven together in order to produce "psychic reality"—starting with fantasy constructions. But if we refrain from systematizing the subject–ego opposition, Jean-Luc Donnet's (1995) formulation about "effects of subjectivation in the ego" seems to me more acceptable than Raymond Cahn's (1991b) invitation to conceive of a "trans-instancial" subject. Indeed, the latter point of view of a subject above the fray is in danger of bringing us back to the good old-fashioned "subject" of philosophy, the same one now used as a weapon by Borch-Jakobsen (2001) in an open attempt to discredit the metapsychological approach.

On the other hand, by conceiving of the subject as an agent of drive (sexual) activity, we are led to recognize in it characteristics proper to the drive, starting with the pulsating way that *active–passive* reversals are linked to *auto–hetero* turning-arounds, within a repeated circularity that engenders both the intermittence of its apparitions and its constant ability to reappear. The experience of sexual desire and the experience of creative inspiration seem in this regard better illustrations for the condition of this subject than the notions of imaginary mastery and power to control that concern the ego. The latter does have the function of maintaining the imaginary unity of the person (modelled on the body) and the feeling of constancy and unity (*self*); but as we know, the ego must often perform this narcissistic function by means of a counter-drive strategy, to serve the pleasure principle.

What freedom?

Once we conceive of the subject function as issuing from the signifying relation within the drive interaction, it is legitimate to wonder what freedom such determinism can leave to the subject in question. Thus, discussing my report, Claudette Lafond, in Montreal, wonders whether this perspective could arrive at "a subjectivity without freedom" (Lafond, 1999).[5] As we know, the psychoanalytic approach is firm in considering psychic phenomena from the angle of their (*Ucs*) *determinism*; because of this it has from the outset exposed itself to stubborn criticism from humanists and philosophers, who reproach it precisely for having conceived of a human being without freedom (delivered over to instinctual movements).

Regarding this difficult question of freedom, a rather comic anecdote comes to mind. In a filmed interview with Lacan in Brussels in the early 1970s, the journalist ended by asking Lacan the famous question: "Lacan, what do say about freedom?" The answer was terse, and accompanied by a rather sarcastic smirk, "Freedom—I never talk about it. . . ."

I would nevertheless point out to Claudette Lafond that in considering signifying determinism as something that alienates freedom, she tends to attribute freedom only to the *imaginary* register (that of the ego). But there are two registers of restricting determinism that must be kept in mind:

- On the one hand, the one that results from the subject's being caught in a *signifying relation*, starting with symbolic interactions with the parental other.
- On the other hand, the issue of alienation in the image of the other, especially in the grip of *identifications*—as is notably the case when there is a *community of disavowal* (Fain, 1982) with a parent.

Having recalled this, I think it can account for the acquisition of *more freedom* in cases like those of Vera and Nicole presented earlier in this book. But I must say that, as a psychoanalyst, I do not envision this increase in freedom as coming from a greater resistance (autonomy) of the ego to drive and signifying determinism; the increase of freedom I think I observe through my practice seems, rather, to consist of the acquisition of a greater margin for *drive play*, which provides more material for subjectivation, through a better capacity for experiencing in a positive way the turnings-around and reversals, especially in a better aptitude for passivation (as a navigator gains more freedom through a better use of the sails in the wind).

An ethics of the psychoanalyst

Any ethics is necessarily founded on a certain conception of the human subject: it is a way of qualitatively taking this subject into account as it is involved in a given practice. Insofar as the psychoanalytic approach is supposed to produce a new and specific involvement of the *subject*, it tends to engender an *ethic* as a consequence—not only in the context of the "classic analysis", but also in the various other modes of effective involvement of a psychoanalyst (in a team, in an institution).

The aim of this book is to show the approach to a subject that issues from a basic relation between the exercise of the *drive* and the play of *signifiers*. As we have seen (chapter 3), subjective appropriation can be built up out of "psychic reality" only through the construction of a *fantasmatic* relationship proper. In doing this, I thought it necessary to insist on the fact—corroborated by material like that presented in chapters 4, 5, and 6—that this notion of "psychic reality" posited by Freud is not primary, natural given, but, rather, is the result of complex psychic work, which may often involve the removal of some parental disavowal. This psychic reality gains from being viewed as the product of a durable "knotting, tying, linking" of the three registers that make up psychic life: the categories of the imaginary, the real, and the symbolic, to which (following Lacan) I have often referred in the above discussion.

Thus Lacan came logically to propose *a formula for fantasy* in which the divided subject (\$)—in fact, what represents it formally—is placed in a certain relationship ($\diamond$) with a representative of the object-cause of desire (a). He puts them together into the relation \$ $\diamond$ a. Let us see how such a formulation could have consequences for the ethic proper to the psychoanalyst, dealing with his or her own specific mode of involvement.

Let us first say that the subjective attitudes of an analyst in the session depend on the idea he or she has of the goal of his or her act. This is no doubt what Michel Neyraut (1974) wanted to show when he revisited the idea, dear to Lacan, that the analyst's "countertransference" logically precedes the patient's transference. The analyst's interest (research), at the start of a treatment, appears as a sort of *offer* to the patient (the offer to transfer), which also has a limit: how far will the analyst go along with it? Lacan actually preferred to speak of the "desire of the analyst" (his desire for analysis), meaning what the analyst expects (more or less consciously) from his practice and the subjective price he is willing to pay for this. The term "countertransference" had earlier been proposed by Freud to designate the analyst's subjective reaction to the *fantasy transference* the patient carries out upon his person. So it is a term that I find incorrect for naming, on the one hand, the first desire (offer) of the analyst that I have just mentioned, and, on the other hand, the phenomenon (described in chapter 6) that tends to occur with patients whose *fantasy appropriation is deficient* and who therefore provoke a kind of induction in the psyche of the therapist, short-circuiting the defensive representative arrangements of the latter.

Going along with the love–hate of the transference

In any case, let us now try to define what sort of ethics could support the analyst's work, if he or she aims to work (for better or for worse) on a better subjectivation of the *drive subject* in his or her analysand. Considering the process of subjectivation as the object *par excellence* of analytic work necessarily has a decisive impact on the particular ethics implicated in this work; Freud shows this very well in the short text entitled "Observations on Transference-Love" (1915a); in which he attempts to defend, in the face of possible criticism from the medical profession, the *respectability* of psychoanalytic practice—especially, of course, the fact that it asks the doctor [sic] to lend himself to his patients' falling in love with him. (Freud speaks only of female patients here—is it because he doesn't dare speak of the male patients' love?)

Freud strives to show that this is a *major technical imperative*, essential to the successful treatment of the neuroses. For it is precisely this thrusting upon the person of said "doctor" in the session of impetuous love (in no way distinguishable, Freud stresses, from any other passionate love in life) that allows one to get a grip on the unconscious register of the psychic determinism that is at work, and to help to undo it.

> It would be easy for me to lay stress on the universally accepted standards of morality and insist that the analyst must never under any circumstances accept to return the tender feelings that are offered him: that, instead, he must consider that the time has come for him to put before the woman who is in love with him the demands of social morality and the necessity for renunciation, and to succeed in making her give up her desires, and, having surmounted the animal side of her self, go on with the work of analysis. . . . I am on this occasion in the happy position of being able to replace the moral embargo

by considerations of analytic technique, without any alteration in the outcome.... To urge the patient to suppress, renounce or sublimate her instincts the moment she has admitted her erotic transference would be, not an analytic way of dealing with them, but a senseless one. It would be just as though, after summoning up a *spirit from the underworld* by cunning spells, one were to send him down again without having asked him a single question. [Freud, 1915a, emphasis added]

Here we find once again the very Freudian image of the "demoniacal" character that the repetition compulsion has—not, of course, because it comes from any physiological *need*, but because it manifests a devilishly stubborn "spirit" (*an unconscious subject?*)

"Psychoanalytic treatment", Freud goes on to say,

is founded on *truthfulness*. In this fact lies a great part of its educative effect and its ethical value. It is dangerous to depart from this foundation.

Anyone who has become saturated in the analytic technique will no longer be able to make use of the lies and pretences which a doctor normally finds unavoidable.... Since we demand strict truthfulness from our patients, we jeopardize our whole authority if we let ourselves be caught out by them in a departure from the truth. [emphasis added]

He concludes:

It is, therefore, just as disastrous for the analysis if the patient's craving for love is gratified as if it is suppressed. [pp. 163–166]

This leads him to say that the analyst must teach his patient to "conquer the pleasure principle" [sic]—in order to acquire a greater interior *"freedom"*. Here then, is the subjective freedom that one is supposed to have to acquire against the pleasure principle.

The analyst must then "lend himself" for a sufficient time to being the object of passionate love—a sexual object for his patient—if he wants to arrive at an effective freeing of her/him as a subject. His position thus has the peculiarity (which sharply distinguishes it from the code of medical morality) that it implies the therapist exposing his person to the neurotic's libidinal fantasy:

the effectiveness of the analysis depends on the aptitude of the one conducting it to occupy the place of *object* of his patient's unconscious desire. Thereafter, the analyst must assume that his interventions emanate from *that very place of the object–cause* and are perceived as such by the patient.

With a patient like the one whose session I reported above—a neurotic who tended to defensively *saturate* the imaginary ego-to-ego relation—the type of intervention I adopted (picking up on the word *"passeur"*, for example) avoids giving too much hold to this imaginary world, allowing it act too much as a lure. After this session, I felt I had more the status of a *partial drive object* (stool–penis) for her and was fairly mistreated as such, without too much reparative imaginary tact. The access to such a register seemed a rather sure indicator of progress towards the liberating accomplishment of the process—insofar as this process must pass through a certain de-idealization of the analyst's overall person.

Lacan's idea that an essential source of the transfer onto the analyst comes from the fact that the latter will occupy, in the patient's eyes, the famous position of the "subject supposed to know" has been rather successful. This presupposition about the other—that he knows—comes from an idealizing imaginary position that is, of course, supposed to exist only in the mind of the patient—indeed, what would we think of an analyst who supposed himself to know what his patient has yet to teach him? . . .

The result of this specific place where the analyst must put himself is a consequent ethic whose imperative is to work towards the emergence of a drive subject, for a certain decision in favour of *passivation* is necessary to accept occupying for his patient the place of *object-cause*—the object designated *little a* by Lacan and defined, as we have seen, as a *real residue* of symbolization, the ineluctable residue from the fact that the human being must put his experience into speech.

The other side of psychoanalysis

This is exactly what Lacan tried to define better in his seminar of 1969–70 entitled *L'envers de la psychanalyse* [The other side of psychoanalysis]. Conceived in the somewhat surrealistic fallout from the movement of May 1968, this seminar is best known as that of "The Four Discourses". In it, indeed, Lacan strove to clarify the specific nature of the psychoanalyst's speech in the session, by confronting it with the characteristics of three other conceivable subjective "discourses": that of the "truth" of the symptom, which he calls the "discourse of the hysteric"; that of the exercise of power, which he calls the "discourse of the master" (the target of political protest); and that of established (academic) knowledge, which he calls "academic discourse", which is equivalent to the discourse of the objective sciences.

Interestingly, the "discourse of the analyst" will, for Lacan, be characterized by the fact that it proffers itself precisely from that very place of the *object (a)*—*cause of desire* and thus *cause of the transference*. It is therefore in contrast with the so-called discourse of the hysteric that comes from the place of the subject ($) of unconscious desire, otherwise referred to as the subject of the symptom. What is proper to the psychoanalyst is thus to conceive of his speech as being tied to that place of the object that is assigned to him by the transference of unconscious desire—the place of an object whose trace is *real* in the psychic apparatus, where it forms a kind of "leftover" that cannot be reduced to discourse. One notes that this central idea of Lacan is placed in the continuation of his seminar on "Ethics" (1959–60), which led, ten years before, to the surprising proposal of a psychoanalytic ethics submitted[6] to the truth that comes from the *id*.

But the fact that the analyst claims to intervene from this obscure place of the *object–cause* entails a twofold mourning on his part: first he must renounce an already established knowledge about the object of his practice and, therefore, accomplish a mourning of the academic or scientific approach; he must also renounce holding a position of power (being master of his patient's destiny, as the hypnotist imagines himself to be, and also the physician). The analyst must rather prepare himself for the possibility that the very accomplishment of his work with the patient will lead him to "fall back" at the end of the treatment, becoming a demystified and now useless object.

On this point, we cannot help but notice that a number of analysts (starting with Lacan himself) seem rather to have worked in their public life, taking back with one hand what they have released with the other through the consensual renunciation in the privacy of their analytic practice. Such recuperation of power (of mastery) can occur especially within psychoanalytic institutions, because of the *debt* that binds young analysts to their training analyst, with all the control that the latter can maintain.

Lacan seems perhaps more consequential in his proposal of an ethics when he rails against an analyst who imagines he could employ attitudes traditionally called those of the "good soul" by moral philosophy, especially in the sense of *understanding empathy*. To put this into the context of what we read in international psychoanalytic publications nowadays, I would just mention the surprise I sometimes feel when certain colleagues make declarations magnifying the effort (of the analysts) to grasp what the patient is "really wanting" to make them understand.

It is clear that here there is no longer any question of an *unconscious* subject (at least in the patient!), and even less, of course, of a *divided* subject. There is only the meritorious effort of the analyst to manage to represent to himself this other ego: the ego of the patient, whose misfortune is that he/she has hitherto only managed to be understood by himself! The practice of the psychoanalyst is thus reduced to the (imaginary) field of the ego-to-ego relation. In other words, it is emptied not only of the notion of the anachronistic restitution brought by the *transference*, but also of what Freud tried to posit as a *meta*(psychological) conception of mental functioning. The notion of the *"ex-centration"* of the psychic apparatus, with the decisive role of a dynamic *Unconscious* as a system proper, seems no longer involved; nor does the Freudian concept of the *drive*—already scuttled by Strachey's decision to reduce Freud's term *Trieb* to "instinct", which has more to do with the behavioural configurations of animals. Such conceptual divergences make one wonder if a common ethic can still be found within an International Psychoanalytical Association, a Babel inhabited by such heterogeneous theoretical references.

But as to the *ethical* position proper to the psychoanalyst, we still must envision that avatar which reappears regularly in our practice: the fact that its setting necessarily fosters an effective sexual or romantic relation. . . . The consequences should, to tell the truth, be damaging only for the process of the analysis itself—as long as, of course, the psychoanalyst, after such a transgression, does not pretend to maintain, in an abusive, perverse way, his "function" as an analyst throughout sessions punctuated by sexual acts. . . . It is, rather, clear from what I have said that the analyst who commits a sexual passage to the act in the session mainly reveals his *inability to sustain his specific desire for analysis*—as if this faltering desire had therefore to be replaced by a stimulant of another order (nature, as we know, abhorring the void . . .)

Such an analyst merely disqualifies himself as an analyst (if not necessarily as a lover), and it seems to me that an Ethics Committee would be obliged to take action in the face of such self-disqualification.

I shall conclude these brief remarks by recalling that the question comes back to the fact that an ethics proper to psychoanalysis is tied up, almost indissociably, with the question of the value of psychoanalysis as a *rigorous approach*, whether or not one wants to call it "scientific" (see the end of chapter 6). The crucial confrontation between *Science* and *Values* (Leibowitz, 1987) dominates the future of research properly called psychoanalytic. But it also dominates the problem of economic competition which is in play in the field of "psychotherapeutic" practices—with conditioning approaches, in particular, that are touted as being both more objectively "scientific" and less costly. . . .

Psychoanalysts at the dawn of the new millennium seem more conscious of being called onto the carpet: they have to sell better their original point of view and its practical implications. Economic pressure compels them to display more clearly *the subjective nature of the object of their activity* and, at the same time, the rigor proper to their specific approach—which unfortunately had been so long "defined" by its formal setting alone: the couch, the frequency, and the duration of the sessions. . . . It is high time now to determine better just what it means to "speak as a psychoanalyst"—in other words, just what is specific to this theoretical and practical approach, through all the various settings (individual, group, institutional) in which it is practiced.

I shall end by suggesting that as psychoanalysts we must above all envision ourselves in the service of something other than an *ortho-psychological* conception aimed at reinforcing the ego's functions by cultivating its illusions of overall unity and mastery. I propose that we consider that the psychoanalyst (among other psychotherapists) is first of all characterized by the fact that his action is motivated by the *passion of the subject of the id*—a subject of drive, a sexually differentiated subject whose qualitative gain is made in the sense of learning how to play better, and especially to *passivate* better, the fruitful structural division that is proper to it.

Temporary recapitulation

Let us now try to bring together the propositions concerning the approach to the subject function, as they have been developed up until now in this book.

▹ The *subject* in the human being issues from *drive activity*; it is first and foremost defined as the *agent* of this drive activity.[7]

▹ From there, the psychic process of subjectivation is fed by the involvement of this subject–agent of the drive in an interaction charged with *meaning*, starting with the responses of the primordial (maternal) partner.

▹ Subjectivation will be nourished chiefly by the *signifying* value of the responses of this parental partner to attempts at getting a drive hold.

▹ Here, what Freud calls a phase of *passivation* of the mode of drive satisfaction will prove decisive, enabling the nascent subject to acquire substance as object of the external drive other (parent) and in this way come to represent itself as a participant in a fantasy relation.

▹ Still, it is necessary for this *other* to authenticate for the subject, in this same movement, the awareness of his/her own *incompleteness*, of the possibility that he/she could *lack* something or be lacking; this is a condition for the representations (word and thing) that are brought back to become *signifiers*—that is, moveable elements in symbolic and subjectivating play.

▹ The fundamental dynamic component of *unbinding* (so-called death drive) should play its role here, so that the subject can become able to *ex-sist* in the libidinal investment of the parental other.

- This takes place notably through a good-enough *sublimation* of the parent's libidinal investment.
- The subject in analysis benefits from experiencing more *passivation* in relation to his/her drive resources and the signifiers that command their interplay.

Notes

1. I first spoke of this patient at the Colloque lyonnais des Arcs on "Le style de l'interprétation", in March 1996.

2. In French, there is an acoustic similarity between *passeur* [ferryman] and *pas-soeur* [non-sister]; it produced a typical mutative signifying effect in this session.

3. The real name of the old ferryman who ferried the dead across the river Styx was Charon. Her slip—"Chiron"—is a second example of a signifying mutation, which the patient could immediately perceive in French, and which performs the same function as Freud attributed to the joke in *Jokes and Their Relation to the Unconscious* (1905c).

4. See the term "Fantasy (UCS)" in *The International Dictionary of Psychoanalysis* (de Mijolla, 2005).

5. Discussion from the Congrès des Psychanalystes de Langue Française, in Paris, May 1999 (Lafond, 1999).

6. The second session Freud reports of his first classical treatment (1909d) is an excellent example of this. In it, Freud declares to the Rat Man that it is not in his power as analyst to exempt the patient from having to restore his fantasy ("he might just as well implore me to exempt him from two comets").

7. See the term "Subject of UCS" in *The International Dictionary of Psychoanalysis* (de Mijolla, 2005).

CHAPTER TEN

The logical stages of subjectivation

The ideas brought together in this last chapter are only meant to provide a sketch, the first steps towards a better psychoanalytic theorization of subjectivation. Since we have conceived of it as emerging *between drive activity and signification*, let us now try to get a better understanding of the process itself.

It is important to see how such subjective development must at every step be carried out in two concurrent registers. On the one hand, there is the *synchronic* relation between "reciprocal subjects" (Lacan, 1945, p. 170), the basic relation with the other-subject, the prototype of which is, of course, the mother–child interaction. But on the other hand, we have the *diachronic* revisiting of the personal history, a temporal path made up of discontinuous "leaps". This second, diachronic register was specifically highlighted by Jacques Lacan when he introduced his notion of *temporal scansion* in the mid-1940s.[1] This new path is thrown into relief in relation to the earlier model, that of the *mirror stage*, suggested by Lacan before the war and taken up again by him in 1949. In fact, with the notion of *scansion*, Lacan means to introduce something of the register of specifically *temporal* succession into what he had until then presented as a model of an *imaginary* structuring relation (i.e., the subject's corporal confrontation with his early parent within the specularity of the "mirror").

This idea of the *mirror* had a very fruitful continuation after the 1950s in D. W. Winnicott's work on what he calls "the mirror-role of the mother in child development". "The precursor of the mirror", says Winnicott (1971b), "is the mother's face." And he adds, "Jacques Lacan's paper, 'Le Stade du Miroir' (1949), has certainly influenced me. He refers to the use of the mirror in each individual's ego development. However, Lacan does not think of the mirror in terms of the mother's face in the way I wish to do here" (p. 111).

Now let us return to Lacan's text, "Le temps logique" [Logical time], which appeared in 1945 shortly after the Liberation in a special issue of *Cahiers d'Art*—a revue that could finally be published again after the "gap" of the war years. This was therefore a historically important issue, and it featured texts by Alquié, Bachelard, Bataille, Char, Eluard, Ponge, Queneau, and reproductions of works by Braque, Kandinsky, Matisse, Picasso, Rouault.... But it is only in 1966, with the publication of *Les Écrits* that this paper (in a much altered version) will become known to a wider audience.

In "Le temps logique", Lacan aims for a better overall understanding of the *relation between time and space* within subjective elaboration—and this long before he had the idea, some twenty years later, of representing psychic construction by means of that deformable (moving) geometry that is *Topology*.[2]

What I shall say here about the process of subjectivation pertains directly to Lacan's introduction in this paper of the notion of the *temporal development of a reciprocal subject in action*. To illustrate this, he uses a well-known problem: that of three prisoners, each of whom has been told that his life would be spared if he could tell the colour of a disk that is on his back and that is invisible to him. Let us recall the elements of this exercise. Each prisoner has a disk fastened to his back; they all know that there were five disks to begin with, *two black and three white*, but, of course, they do not know the colour of the two disks that have been set aside; they have no way of perceiving the disk they are wearing, though they can see the disks of the other two; and they cannot communicate with each other.

In the problem recounted here, it is said that after long consideration, observing that the disks of the other two prisoners are white, the three prisoners finally make a nearly simultaneous move towards the exit. Thus they leave *together*, each one having concluded that he was wearing a white disk. The thought process of any one of them may be summed up as follows: given that I can see that my two companions are whites, I think that *if I were a black*, each of the other two could say to himself that if he were also a black, the third one, seeing two blacks before him would know immediately that he was a white and would leave. However, neither of them is leaving; from this, each one will deduce that he is a white and leave (neither one leaves, therefore I am not a black). There is a lengthy reflexive suspense until each one, seeing two whites before him, feels he has confirmation for his conclusion—"*I myself am white like the others*"—and all three finally decide to leave.

But Lacan qualifies as *sophism* this condensed way of showing the path to each one's indirect recognition of his own colour. Indeed, Lacan believes that it glosses over the essential point: that the access to a subjective certitude through the other can only be attained by way of *two successive and suspensive temporal "scansions"*—two stops and two starts.

So he takes up again the decomposition of the logical process, first from the point of view of one of the characters, called A, who must come to a conclusion using his perception of the two others and their responses as a guide. The way towards resolution of the subjective incertitude can effectively begin, as we have already seen, with the idea that A, seeing B and C are white, will first hypothesize that he is black and is seen as such by the two others.

He then tries to imagine what B might be saying to himself when he sees, hypothetically, that A is black and C is white: B could first suppose that he himself is also black and tell himself that C, seeing two blacks before him, would leave without further delay, certain that he is white since there are only two blacks. Now, B sees that C does not leave, and this tells him that C is not looking at two blacks.

We have seen how A's reasoning, starting from the hypothesis that he is black (and that B and C see that he is black) thus comes to consider that if this were the case and that, nevertheless, C does not leave, B would have to conclude that he himself is not black, which would enable him to leave right away.

Now, we see that *neither C nor B leave;* therefore, B has not been able to derive from the fact that C does not leave (A still being supposed to be black) that he himself is white. A can consequently say to himself: if B does not leave, it must be because he sees I am not black; my initial hypothesis is therefore false, and I can leave with the certainty that I am white.

Since each of the three has gone through the same reasoning, they finally decide to make a move to leave at the same time. It is at this point that Lacan rectifies the "logical error" that he calls "*a sophism*". For each one, seeing the two others make a move to leave, cannot help but *doubt* this certainty again, since it is precisely on the two others' attitude of expectation and immobility that his conviction was based. This conviction must necessarily be shaken by the others' moving towards the exit with him. A must then stop to reconsider his deduction on the basis of this new information comprised of the others' move towards the exit. But here his cogitation will be enriched by a new fact: *the two others also stop when they see him suspend his movement!* ...

So A has stopped leaving—this is the first stop or "suspensive scansion"—and he must try again to think as B might. He can tell himself that the latter is perhaps a little slow-witted and took some time to understand that if A is black and C does not leave, he himself can only be white. In which case, then, A is really black and was about to make the fatal mistake of leaving to declare that he is white.... But seeing the others stop at the same time as he, A tells himself that if B really saw that he was black, *the fact that A stopped would not alter his decision.* If A's stopping makes B doubt, it is because the latter thinks he is the same colour (and so does C).

A then decides to start again towards the exit to announce that he is white, and the two others immediately go with him. As the stakes are high (their lives will be spared only if they are not mistaken about their colour), it is understandable that A would again need a moment of reflexive pause—this is the second stop or "suspensive scansion". He wonders if it is the same as before: are they caught up in a cycle of indefinite repetition?

Although he sees the two others stop with him, A can now understand that a *logical progress* has occurred for him in relation to the previous scansion. For if A's first stop ought not to have made B (or C) hesitate if A were really black, it would be even less likely, if A were black, that B would have stopped a second time!

This time A can tell himself: "if B always hesitates at the same time I do, it means that he does not see that I am black but that I am white like him, which leads him *to reason as I do*." And all three go out, in a hurry to conclude.

In sum, we see that the diachronic development proposed by Lacan does not modify the concrete elements of the condensed solution to the problem as it has first been presented. But the temporal scansions that he shows aim to emphasize what he calls "the instances of time in logical progress"—to mark the necessary steps towards the achievement of subjective certitude about one's own colour (suggested, of course, as a metaphor for self-knowledge) and attest to the performance of a true experiment. This leads Lacan to characterize the different successive moments in the following way: he calls the first "the time of seeing" (observing that the two others are white), the second "the time of understanding" (cogitation leading to the first move to leave and the first scansion), and the third "the time of concluding" (with the second scansion permanently removing the subjective doubt).

This experimental model is valuable in that it shows two essential reference points that command the progress of any subjectivation—but this will be even more explicit in the finished version published in *Écrits* in 1966, along with the specifically Lacanian contribution of *signifying scansion*.

The first point is that the temporal scansion presented by Lacan is fundamentally inspired by the Freudian notion of *"après-coup"* (*deferred action*; e.g. 1918b [1914])—and it is surprising to note how this notion continues to be disregarded by many English-language psychoanalysts. With his *deferred action*, Freud already effectively introduces the temporal dimension in a way that comes close to that of *logical time*. We know, for example, that what he calls "castration" is conceived by him as a subjective experience also necessitating several stages. First, there is the time of simple perception—the time when one sees that the penis is absent in the woman (the time of seeing); but this will then acquire its full charge of signification, giving rise to anxiety about losing the penis and organizing the castration complex, with its symptomatic avatars, only at later moments, such as when a parent threatens the child because of his masturbatory activity. Freud considers that the signification given to the experience will be changed as a succession of certain events occur later, gradually modifying the implications that may be subjectively derived from it. The diachronic dimension is thus introduced as a series of experiences in the form of ruptures, transforming leaps, and subjective discontinuities having a retroactive effect.

The second point, however, is that each step of the process is also defined in terms of *synchronic causality*. Indeed, Lacan says that the illustrative story of the three prisoners allows us to posit that "this subjectivation is that of a reciprocal subject in action". It is from the behavioural response of the game's protagonists that each one's imaginary suppositions will be able to gain certitude. The subjectivation of the three "whites" can advance only through each one's *hurry to conclude*, and it attains a quality of certitude (of full psychic reality) only at the moment of their last move to leave.

Here we again meet with one of Freud's essential reference points, having to do with the early drive interaction as a matrix for subjective determination in everyone (chapter 1). Exchanges between mother and child appear to be the prototype of this. Now, Freud did not fail to note the occurrence of *successive times* within early drive exchanges. Thus in "Instincts and Their Vicissitudes" (1915c), he envisions a succession of active, auto-erotic, and passive modes of drive satisfaction. And it is during the time of *passivation* of the aim, when satisfaction is sought in a passive way (to get oneself looked at, to get oneself handled) that the quality of the response of the exterior subject (the maternal protagonist in the first drive circuit) will play a decisive role in the constitution of subjective experience.

The conjunction of two dimensions, synchronic and diachronic, helps us to grasp that subjectivation involves the *transformation of a spatial element* (body-to-body confrontation) *within the dimension of time*. The temporal dimension takes on its own reality through a series of performed acts (departures, stops) constituting different *responses from the protagonist* that provoke what Lacan calls *scansions*.

Within this perspective, the Freudian concept of *"transference"* takes on full meaning. It is the revisiting in the treatment, repetitively at first, and in an anachronistic and compulsive way, of certain early experiences that are difficult to subjectivate. Going back to them in the treatment tends to comprise a number of *logical times*, in which the experience is gradually transformed. But this also entails that the response from the analyst–protagonist will intervene as a decisive element in the subjective quality of the experience in question. Here there must be enough *reciprocity* in play, as well as enough reversibility, which comes back to the basic notion of a permutation of positions (active–passive) within the drive interaction.

Finally, it is essential to place the preceding notions about *logical time* within the context of the genesis of Lacan's fundamental distinction of the registers of the real, the imaginary, and the symbolic, which he first spoke of in 1953 (Lacan, 2006, p. 671). The symbolic register, obviously decisive in the process of subjectivation, literally issues forth from the notion of *signifier*; so we should now clarify some implications of the idea of *signifier*.

Signifying scansions

It is only in his 1966 publication that Lacan will use the term *signifier* to designate *scansions*. This concept of the signifier comes, in fact, from the idea of *unary line*, such as it was developed in Lacan's 1961 seminar "Identification" (as yet unpublished), where he tells his listeners about a "discovery" he has just made, at the Museum of Prehistory in Saint-Germain-en-Laye. Lacan speaks of how moved he was to see a reindeer rib, dating from the Palaeolithic era (c. 30,000 BC), on which could be seen a whole series of small nicks, like some kind of tally (bookkeeping).

Beyond the emotion he felt at imagining this old ancestral subject at work, Lacan declares that he was struck by something that seemed absolutely evident: these little lines all in a row, despite their similarity and repetition, *mark a difference* (in an accounting, perhaps).

He then says that "this sameness is constituted of exactly this: that the signifier as such connotes difference in its pure state". This leads him to consider that the nature of the signifier is precisely to introduce discontinuity. Lacan posits that: "the peculiarity of the signifier is that it introduces a discontinuity into the real" (Lacan, 1960b, p. 678). It is this notion of discontinuity that, for Lacan, characterizes the specific psychic register he calls the *symbolic*, differentiating it from the category of the imaginary—that of synchronic corporal representations. Thus the signifier will be characterized like this: *something happens at a given moment that was not known in advance*. This moment of event-response, says Lacan, is precisely that of the *scansion*. At this "stop", a fundamental difference is produced within the very function of synchronous determinism: the space of difference wherein subjectivation can occur. It is, notably, the moment of the analyst's interpretative reaction that introduces a difference into the pure repetition compulsion.

Here Lacan returns to his idea that the agent of the drive is initially "acephalic" (that is, instinctual, properly speaking). This, as we have seen (chapter 1) characterizes a baby's first signals (of need) at the outset, *before the response from the other-subject* (*the parent*). This "pre-subjective" state is like that of prisoner A at the moment (phase 1) when he can visually perceive only that the two others are white—that is, before he can give a meaning to their behaviour (response). It is also the state of the little boy who happens to observe with his own eyes the simple fact of his sister's lack of a penis, before an adult has signified to him the threat of losing the penis if he uses it for forbidden purposes. Thus the process of personal subjectivation constitutes a complex relational one that includes meaningful (parental) responses provided little by little over the course of his development—and when we speak of processes, we are obviously speaking of a dynamic of transformations.

This brings to mind the notion of *unbinding* (chapter 8), for it would seem that the role of what Freud (1920g) called the "death drive" accounts, from a *dynamic* point of view, for this signifying notion of discontinuity. After the time for seeing (which may still be one of fusion), the time for understanding and, above all, the time for concluding introduce a necessary *subjective unlinking*. The etymology of the word "decision", as Eric Porge (1989) points out, reminds us that to decide is to cut, to make a "de-schism". Unbinding is, in fact, an essential contribution to the process.

The manifest subject in the image, and the latent-absent subject in the act

From the point of view of the Freud's "second metapsychology" (Roussillon, 1995)—that of *Beyond the Pleasure Principle* (1920g), introducing the *death drive*—I would like to emphasize how the process of subjectivation can work through a treatment, starting with "manifest" material of certain symptoms (in the sessions or between sessions) that are more or less characterized by this discontinuity.

We know how the dreamwork *disguises* latent thoughts beneath manifest figures, which in fact *translate* complex thought processes into primary images through condensation and displacement. This is what Freud showed through his analysis of dream formations and neurotic symptoms.

But such a relationship between manifest and latent does not always indicate that a process of subjectivation has been achieved. In our psychoanalytic practice, we have to take into account a remarkable variety of registers of manifest symptomatic elements. Among the many clinical examples with which we are confronted, there are cases where the analyst is solicited in a register of manifest expression one might call *visceral*, and which leads one to speak of *something latent that goes back to something unrepresentable*[3] (see also chapter 6).

The great diversity of cases we have to treat obliges us to consider that what is "presented as manifest" in the session by a patient can refer back to causal traces made of very different stuff. There may, of course, be verbal images or thing-representations, but also bodily sensations or acted behaviours. . . . Through the diversity itself, we must observe that the potential for *significance* (and therefore subjectivation) of these manifest elements can prove to be quite variable—as may be, by the same token, their ability to serve the patient's work of perlaboration, in the sense of better restoring the *existential suffering* that afflicts him.

To illustrate how different kinds of symptomatic material may differ in their ability to serve the process of subjectivation, I shall give two brief excerpts from the treatments of two very different patients—who were nevertheless both strongly committed to an analytic process that they invest in a very personal way, and who are both capable of producing very fine perlaborative work.

The Oedipus complex: here we go again . . .

The first patient is a South American man, a functionary, who has already done a long personal analysis in his native country before being posted to Paris. He then seeks me out in order to start a new treatment in French. After a few weeks with four sessions per week, I start telling myself that I'm dealing with the kind of neurotic we hardly see nowadays. His restrictive phobic–obsessive symptoms were surely *loosened up*, but they perhaps were also *maintained* by what he gives me to understand was very understanding support from his previous analyst, a South American woman, who showered him with comforting talk.

One day, he tells me of an adventure he had the day before: he managed to have sex with a "professional woman" whom he phoned and asked to come over to his house. He describes this lady as "very brutal" and even "monstrous". At the same time I can detect that "sweet, friendly girls" actually make him feel much more inhibited.

So I decide to call his attention to the fact that he had applied the same adjective—*monstrous*—to his mother in our preliminary interviews, when he was trying to describe her bossy, intrusive, and overbearing behaviour throughout his whole youth.

At the next session, he recounts a dream in which *he sees himself telling his brother he has AIDS, but where at the same time he has the impression that his brother could also have AIDS.* He explains that AIDS is "manifested" [sic] in his dream in the following way: in the foreground he sees his own feet, swollen, with a red mark on both sides of each ankle, "like a hole". His associations lead him to mention vaguely the idea of a "punishment" in consequence of his sexual adventure with the "monstrous" professional (here he assures me that he took all the necessary precautions).

Finally, it occurs to me to ask this anxious man if he knows the literal meaning of the word *"oedipus"* in Greek.[4] And in fact, the interpretative grasp of this (manifest) image of *swollen, pierced feet* will help him make progress in acknowledging his (latent) incestuous erotic fixation on his mother.

In sum, we have here material from a classical treatment where the work of subjectivation can be developed with just some leverage from the dream's signifying representation.

The bad subject of absence

Something else again is the practical impact of symptoms in the form of *acting out*, which for a long time repetitively suspended (scanned) the treatment of another patient that I had nevertheless seen at the outset as an analysand as gifted as the first.

He is also a man in his thirties, and quite good-looking. He comes to consult me because of *repetitive break-ups* of his relationships, both professional and romantic. He tells me that both kinds are attractive and promising at first, but then they break up, for one reason or another, and lead to "a total loss", as he puts it.

This man, whom I will call Antonio, is from a very poor background. He was born in the south of Italy, of a father who was a humble craftsman and who had often worked illegally in Paris for periods of time—so that Antonio was placed in a kind of orphanage in their home region for all of his latter childhood.

He would receive unexpected visits from his mother, who never saw any reason to warn him when she'd be coming, and this about three times a year; but never from his father, whom he would see again only in preadolescence when he could finally leave the orphanage and go to live with his parents, who were then more settled in Paris.

Antonio speaks French without an accent. He explains that he could accomplish his university education thanks to an extremist political organization in which he has chosen to become a militant; in this way he has acquired a certain economic and legal competence. His bilingualism underlies a rather wide general culture, and he shows *insight* and a certain analytic perspicacity.

The analytic work starts off at a bi-weekly rhythm, and he pays me punctually despite his precarious financial situation. At first he talks very much about his relationship with his son, whom he had with a French woman older than himself, with whom he is going through a lengthy divorce. He notes that his son is now at the age when he himself was *placed* in the orphanage, and also the extent to which his own experience of abandonment has been reactivated by his now being separated from his son.

But after a few months, Antonio unexpectedly stops coming to his sessions. I suppose that he has *fled into the cure*, for both his professional and matrimonial situations are fairly improved. But he will nevertheless re-contact me about three months later, apologizing very much. On the telephone he tells me that he was afraid I would refuse to see him again.

So he will return, telling me about his difficult life as a divorced father, and an expatriate between two countries, and about the persistent, virulent conflict between him and his ex-wife. He says he needs to come back to "work" with me on this dimension of his relationship with her that he sees as "hateful". Soon he will associate this with the formidable ambivalence of his relation with his father. He informs me that he has worked "illegally" for his father during times when he himself was unemployed.

The family relations that this patient tells me about remind me very much of those in the extraordinary novels of John Fante,[5] striking in the funny-pathetic way they depict how impossible it can be for a son to make his father own up to the problems of his own behaviour—unbearably abusive, destructive, and truculent. . . .

And then Antonio will disappear again for several months, without warning me in the least. The *acting out* in the transference is very clear, and I feel irritated with him. But he will once again telephone a few months later, apparently feeling confused, to explain that he now has a legal practice "straddling" his home country and France, and from which position he intends to take clever advantage of the future European Community. He declares that he needs to see me more than ever now and asks if I would agree to schedule his sessions near weekends, when he comes to Paris to see his son.

But this new resumption of the treatment will enable me to see that some psychic progress has been made: *it is not just a repetition of the same*. This patient is living through a "logical process" that transforms his subjectivity. Given that he is relatively well off now financially, he will be able to focus work in analysis more on his family conflicts (with his parents, his siblings, and his son's mother). He decides to settle down officially in his home country during the work week, and to live there with a new woman, who is herself the mother of two daughters whose father is serving a life-term in prison for terrorism.

But I will once again have to endure another disappearance on his part, lasting several months; after which he will re-contact me to talk about the conditions for picking up yet again. This new straying will confirm my idea that this behaviour—as "manifest" as it gets, in a sense—must be considered as coming from repetition compulsion, in the Freudian sense of *Wiederholungszwang*. The process of this treatment will thus follow a course that begins with a revisiting in the present (of the act) of what had so strongly marked this patient's childhood: the primary print of parental presences and absences, which could not be psychically integrated—going so far as to reproduce the more or less thrice-yearly appearances–disappearances of his mother! . . .

By analogy I think of another patient, a woman, who for a long time behaved in a similarly disconcerting way with me, turning around a sort of *insolvability*: she wrote me a series a checks that bounced; each time she would make prompt *reparations*, apologizing profusely. . . .

When she was a little girl she had effectively been abandoned by parents who were incapable of taking care of her; social services could find nothing better to do than place her in a home for "retarded" children, in the Massif Central region—until her grandparents finally decided to take her to live with them. After she had been in treatment long enough—and had committed enough *acting out*—this woman was able to procure a good job; she was able to re-establish a relationship with her mother, who was living in a community in the Orient; but she could never manage to make her father "be present", even in a symbolic way. . . .

It seems to me that treatments like this allow us better to detect certain mechanisms at work in the very foundations of the process of subjectivation.

1. We gradually see the patient appropriating mentally (subjectivating) a phenomenon on the order of the re-actualization, through acted repetition by him/her in the treatment, of something he/she had to endure in early life. A certain *failure to represent it* undoubtedly explains the acted compulsion to inflict it upon the analyst, placed in a position to endure it. With his unexpected appearances and disappearances, Antonio establishes himself at the start as the *manifest agent*, but one that is somewhat *acephalic* (in the "time for seeing"). Then, through the re-actualizations of this drama, something like a self-attributing turnabout will develop in the patient, allowing for the gradual subjectivation of *it*—that which has happened, but which has not been sufficiently experienced, as Winnicott (1971a) put it so well. Before this treatment could proceed normally (without more acted-out break-ups), three years of repeated acting out had to pass. But could this have been avoided?
2. A symptomatic apparition of this kind is very different from a return of the repressed. There was not really any *amnesia* on Antonio's part about the events he endured as a child; it was just that their signifying charge remained as though clamped down by a narcissistic defence in the form of a disavowal of absence (Penot, 1989).

It seems that the gradual removal in this treatment of a certain lack of representation of absence necessitated that the analyst accept *passivation*. This entails suspending as much as possible the *attributive judgement* in accepting to endure what was inflicted without suppressing it in the manner of a superego—the analyst must be animated instead by the idea that *this* holds the key to the process of this particular analysis. One could see this as an illustration of a process of symbolization developing by means of acted *scansions* whose reiteration will gradually advance a certain *suspension* of signification.

3. I was also able to participate in the patient's gradually grasping of the *metaphorical* import of his manifest symptom, whose implications for signification in terms of the outcome became clearer as the process of symbolization of the symptomatic content went on. In terms of Freud's "first topic", this could be described as the building up of the *Unconscious* system—in which the problematic character of early events had short-circuited the symbolic play that should give structure to the subject.

4. In this a way a certain type of "manifest" material (whether delusive, behavioural, or somatic) will attest to a defect of *primary symbolization* in the psychic organization of the patient, which has been mooted by what cannot be represented. This is also the case, I believe, with those patients who bring *perverse* attitudes to bear on their treatment, placing the analyst in the difficult position of having to support (passivate) a transference interaction that is narcissistically very trying. But this seems to be the only kind of *transference* these patients are capable of, and it is through this that they must acquire a better ability to represent to themselves their career as a suffering subject.

A case like that of Antonio shows, above all, that a revisiting of a defective primary symbolization must be accomplished by putting a sufficient amount of *intersubjectivity* into play. This ties in with how a psychoanalyst's practice with troubled youngsters can be: the therapist cannot avoid a certain amount of *acting* and *endurance*—especially when the *acting out* is coming from the therapist him/herself!

So it is as if the acquisition of a capacity for primary symbolization had to result, for some "borderline" analysands (as for the young children), from a dialectic of mutual acknowledgement of drive interactions and their attributing reversals.

The practice of a psychoanalyst in a large city nowadays keeps confronting him or her with patients for whom this *acted* dimension appears, at least at the beginning, to be the prevalent mode of symptomatic expression. Such dispositions are characteristic of what are commonly called "borderline states" (see chapter 8). The style of the treatments of such patients—whatever their age—makes them resemble the treatments of adolescents, in that the process of subjectivation manifests itself in its "nascent" state—that is, precisely through the act. But this tends to sorely test the analyst's capacity for *passivation*.

The acted scansion

The Lacanian notion of scansion is, as we have said, inseparable from the idea of a subjectivating act. This given has had some grave consequences, as we know, on the practice of psychoanalysis in France.

The real heart of this historic drama was played out between 1953 and 1964, between Lacan and the societies belonging to the International Psychoanalytical Association. The latter was never willing to ratify the inflection Lacan gave to his practice, which favoured an interpretive activity precisely in the form of *acted scansion* (for example, sending the patient away the moment he says something important, instead of at the time the session is scheduled to end). Thus began the painful controversy over Lacan's famous *short sessions*—an issue that even now divides the vast constellation of psychoanalysts known as "Lacanian". Patrick Guyomard recalled this at a talk given to the Paris Psychoanalytical Society, suggesting that we consider that there are two "sorts" of Lacanians: on the one hand, those who continue to subscribe to the logic of the *scansion* as a psychoanalyst's act *par excellence*, and to the logic of *la passe*[6] as the way of affirming its quality; and, on the other hand, "the others" whose modes of practice are similar to those of French-speaking analysts belonging to the International Psychoanalytical Association.

I will say here that, in my opinion, the essential flaw in the option favouring *acted scansion* (and the short session that comes with it) is that it freezes the analytic act into a gross distortion: in fact, it tends to *impose in a systematic way an exaggerated, one-sided dis-symmetry wherein the analyst is always active, and the patient is always passively enduring, and the roles are never reversed*. In the light of some of the perspectives presented in this book, it would seem that, in its very one-sidedness and uniformity, this position is literally *perverse*, for it hampers the necessary turnabouts–reversals that characterize the progress of ordinary drive vicissitudes and, through it, the process of subjectivation.

Such systematic hyperactivity on the part of the analyst resembles that of pathogenic parents—like the mother one can imagine Vera had (chapter 2). This attitude flagrantly contradicts essential points of Lacan's own theoretical work, notably where it tries to specify the singular position of the analyst operating as object-cause of the transference. Perhaps we have here a particularly blatant historical example (there are plenty of others!) of lasting contradiction between the defensive behaviour of an author (especially in his *horror of passivity*, to use Freud's term) and the conceptual fecundity of the theoretical perspectives he opened up. Especially that what is peculiar to the analyst's singular position implies logically and necessarily an *ethics of reciprocal passivation*—which I hope most of the clinical examples in this book have been able to show.

In a later seminar, "The Logic of Fantasy" (1966–67, unpublished), Lacan worked further on the issue of the act as founder of the subject. He postulates that the act (the patient's!) is a vehicle for something of the repetition and that the signifier's role is to serve as the support *par excellence* of this repetition. *The repetition has a sort of link with the signifier*. Here we see Lacan placing himself into a critical rupture with the thesis advanced by Freud in "Remembering, Repeating and Working-Through" (1914g). Lacan will notably declare this: "The act is the founder of the subject. The act is precisely the equivalent of the repetition by itself.... It is itself the double loop [Moebius strip] of the signifier.... What is the effect of the act? It is the labyrinth proper to the recognition of its effects by a subject who cannot recognize it [its effect], because—as subject—it is totally transformed by the act. The subject is, in the act, represented as pure division...."

Here Lacan comes back to the idea of the human subject as essentially "divided". This leads him, in his seminar of that year, to a rather radical subversion of the Cartesian *cogito*, trying to show, with brio as convincing as it is disturbing, that "I am where

I don't think" and "I am not where I think". Going back to the L Schema (chapter 9), we see that in each of these two propositions, one of the two *Is* can be replace by the term *ego* (and vice versa).

This division of the human subject had previously been represented by Lacan under another aspect: that of the opposition between subject of the utterance and subject of the statement—which he notably formalized with two stages of his *graph of desire*.[7]

In the end, it seems to me, these successive models proposed by Lacan have the advantage of being able to represent, each in its own way, a way of accounting for the impossibility for a human subject of attaining an overall grasp of his subjective knowledge. No subject can *globalize* his subjective experience—be for himself a complete *self*. This leads the psychoanalyst to the fundamental consideration that the human subject, as an agent of the drive, on the one hand, and as the product of a signifying relation in which he is inter-acted, on the other hand, cannot ever really experience himself as *one*, contrary to what the ego tends to imagine itself structurally, taking the body as its model.[8]

The passivation of the psychoanalyst subject

The moment has come to conclude this book, temporarily at least, for I intend to continue the study of the process of subjectivation at work *on both sides* of the psychoanalytic relation—insofar as it is the heart of this and is what best defines its specific methodology and rigor.

On the analyst's side, we will have to define better what it means to *think and speak as a psychoanalyst* (about a patient's treatment, first of all). Indeed, this is now an essential socio-political issue throughout the different settings in which our practice may intervene: in what terms should the psychoanalyst's activity be defined, especially in relation to all the other sorts of psychotherapeutic modes, whether or not these use the body.[9]

We must first acknowledge the conceptual poverty that could lead us to settle for a definition of the psychoanalytic treatment in terms of the operative arrangement of the couch and the formal minimum of four sessions per week! . . . We know perfectly well that genuine psychoanalytic work can be carried out within other settings, starting, of course, with face-to-face individual sessions, but also within analytic psychodrama, and even through analytic teamwork within an institution.

What I have said about subjectivation has much to do with the fact that practices other than that of the *classical analysis* give more signifying importance to the *acts* of the patient, not just to his speech. It is particularly important to me to stress that *psychoanalytic teamwork*—which is especially indicated in the treatment of grave disorders of subjectivation, which require admission to a day-hospital—is especially apt to proving the relevance of the "synchronic" model discussed above, and it makes one recognize as a basic condition of subjectivation the decisive putting into play of a dynamic of *reciprocal subjects*.

Though it is no doubt essential to admit that psychoanalytic work can be carried out in practical conditions other than those of the classical treatment, I think it is false to speak of "applications" of psychoanalysis. This term sounds a false and condescending note; for we can observe that it is now, rather, at the limits of the "classical treatment" that psychoanalysis tends to learn the most, that it can increase or even rectify its theories and thus remain alive. The sort of smugness this term carries tends to trivialize and even mask what in fact tends to be the most creative aspect of psychoanalytic research: the areas of its activity through which it gains new acquisitions, precisely those where it has to deal with major deficits of subjectivation. It would not be absurd to think that it is in large part by working in this area that psychoanalysis could perhaps be able to respond to the needs of the twenty-first century, with the increase in "borderline" pathologies dominated by acting and the accompanying decline in *repression*.

This said, we cannot fail, in conclusion, to recall the basic references that define the psychoanalytic approach—what Freud called the "fundamental concepts"[10]—which must guide its action and differentiate it from other therapeutic practices relating to psychology. For Freud, the fundamental concepts are notably those of *drive, the Unconscious, repetition compulsion,* and *transference*. Now, it must be noted that at present many psychoanalysts, however attached they may be to their sacrosanct four-sessions-per-week, speak of their clinical work as though it no longer had much to do with these parameters, which are nevertheless what enable us to distinguish the psychoanalytic approach (as *meta*) from the practice of a kind of normative psychology.

Notes

1. I have been considerably aided in this by Eric Porge's careful work, *Se compter trois* (1989), to which I would like to pay tribute here.
2. Analysts interested in furthering their understanding of Lacan should consult the *Introductory Dictionary of Lacanian Psychoanalysis* (Dylan, 1996).
3. The "unrepresentable" [*L'irréprésentable*] is the theme of Volume 1 of the *Revue Française de Psychanalyse* in 1992.
4. The meaning of *oedipus* is both "swollen feet" and "knowledge".
5. I am thinking in particular of *The Brotherhood of the Grape* (Fante, 1977)
6. It is important to recall that Lacan himself—when he still had his wits about him—declared in 1978–79 that the experiment of *"la passe"* that he had earlier promoted, in 1967, for certifying psychoanalysts of his École freudienne had been a failure.
7. I have commented on this elsewhere (Penot, 1995).
8. This structural division of the subject is manifest in the plurality of each person's genetic lines (paternal, maternal, . . .), concretized in the heterogeneity of each pair of chromosomes. One wonders, with some anxiety, whether a *subject* could result from the process of human cloning.
9. Paul Israël (1999) has written on this issue.
10. It is always interesting to reread Freud closely. At the beginning of his decisive work on "Instincts and Their Vicissitudes" (1915c), he is careful to declare that "The advance of knowledge, however, does not tolerate any rigidity even in definitions. Physics furnishes an excellent illustration of the way in which even 'basic concepts', that have been established in the form of definitions, are constantly being altered in their content" (p. 117).

REFERENCES

Anzieu, D. (1989). *The Skin Ego*. New Haven, CT: Yale University Press.
Arfouilloux, J.-C. (1999). Un sujet de passion. *Revue Française de Psychanalyse, 63* (5, special issue): 1565–1569.
Balier, C. (2002). *Psychanalyse des comportements sexuels violents*. Paris: Presses Universitaire de France.
Bergeret, J. (1986). Etats limites et leurs aménagements. In: *Psychologie pathologique*. Paris: Masson.
Bion, W. R. (1967). *Second Thoughts: Selected Papers on Psychoanalysis*. London: Heinemann.
Borch-Jacobsen, M. (2001). *Le sujet freudien*. Paris: Flammarion.
Botella, C., & Botella, S. (2001). Figurabilité et régrédience. *Revue Française de Psychanalyse, 65* (5, special issue): 1149.
Braunschweig, D., & Fain, M. (1971). *Eros et Anteros*. Paris: Payot.
Cahn, R. (1991a). *Adolescence et folie—les déliaisons dangereuses*. Paris: Presses Universitaire de France, Le fil rouge.
Cahn, R. (1991b). Le sujet. *Revue Française de Psychanalyse*, 55 (6): 1353.
Chabert, C. (1999). Les voies intérieures. *Revue Française de Psychanalyse, 63* (5, special issue): 1445–1488.
Chasseguet-Smirgel, J. (1973). L'idéal du moi. *Revue Française de Psychanalyse, 37* (5/6, special issue): 735–929.

Damourette, J., & Pichon, E. (1946). *Des mots à la pensée. Essai de grammaire de la langue française.* Paris: Vrin.

Debray, R. (1999). Aléas de l'accès à la position passive. *Revue Française de Psychanalyse, 63* (5, special issue): 1785.

de Mijolla, A. (Ed.) (2005). *International Dictionary of Psychoanalysis.* Detroit, MI: Thomson Gale.

Denis, P. (1997). *Emprise et satisfaction.* Paris: Presses Universitaire de France, Le fil rouge.

Diatkine, G. (2000). Le surmoi culturel [Rapport pour le Soixantième Congrès des Psychanalystes de Langue Française, Montréal]. *Revue Française de Psychanalyse, 64* (5, special issue): 1523–1588.

Diatkine, R. (1995). *Pourquoi on m'a né?* Paris: Calmann-Levy.

Didier-Weill, A. (1998). *Invocations.* Paris: Calmann-Levy.

Donnet, J.-L. (1995). L'opération méta, In: *Le divan bien tempéré.* Paris: Presses Universitaire de France, p. 281.

Dylan, E. (1996). *An Introductory Dictionary of Lacanian Psychoanalysis.* New York: Routledge.

Fain, M. (1882). *Le désir de l'interprète.* Paris: Aubier Montaigne.

Fante, J. (1977). *The Brotherhood of the Grape.* Edinburgh: Canongate.

Freud, S. (1895d). *Studies on Hysteria. S.E. 2.*

Freud, S. (1900a). *The Interpretation of Dreams, S.E. 4*, p. 5.

Freud, S. (1905c). *Jokes and Their Relation to the Unconscious. S.E. 8.*

Freud, S. (1908c). On the sexual theories of children. *S.E. 9*, p. 216.

Freud, S. (1909b). Analysis of a phobia in a five-year-old boy. *S.E. 10*, p. 3.

Freud, S. (1909d). Notes upon a case of obsessional neurosis. *S.E. 10*, p. 155.

Freud, S. (1911b). Formulations on the two principles of mental functioning. *S.E. 12*, p. 220 fn.

Freud, S. (1911c [1910]). Psycho-analytic notes on an autobiographical account of a case of paranoia (Dementia paranoides). *S.E. 12*, p. 3.

Freud, S. (1914c). On narcissism: An introduction. *S.E. 14*, p. 94.

Freud, S. (1914g). Remembering, repeating and working-through. *S.E. 12*, p. 145.

Freud, S. (1915a). Observations on transference-love. *S.E. 12*, p. 163.

Freud, S. (1915c). Instincts and their vicissitudes. *S.E. 14*, p. 117.

Freud, S. (1915d). Repression. *S.E. 14*, p. 141.

Freud, S. (1915e). The unconscious. *S.E. 14*, p. 166.

Freud, S. (1918b [1914]). From the history of an infantile neurosis. *S.E. 17*, p. 3.

Freud, S. (1919e). A child is being beaten. *S.E. 17*, p. 181.
Freud, S. (1919h). The uncanny. *S.E. 17*, p. 219.
Freud, S. (1920a). The psychogenesis of a case of homosexuality in a woman. *S.E. 18*, p. 147.
Freud, S. (1920g). *Beyond the Pleasure Principle. S.E. 18*, p. 7.
Freud, S. (1921c). *Group Psychology and the Analysis of the Ego. S.E. 18*, p. 69.
Freud, S. (1923b). *The Ego and the Id. S.E. 19*, p. 3.
Freud, S. (1924b [1923]). Neurosis and psychosis. *S.E., 19*, p. 151.
Freud, S. (1924c). The economic problem of masochism. *S.E. 19*, p. 159.
Freud, S. (1925h). Negation. *S.E. 19*, p. 235.
Freud, S. (1925j). Some psychical consequences of the anatomical distinction between sexes. *S.E. 19*, p. 252.
Freud, S. (1930a [1929]). *Civilization and its Discontents. S.E. 21*, p. 267.
Freud, S. (1937d). Constructions in analysis. *S.E. 23*, p. 267.
Freud, S. (1950[1895]). Project for a scientific psychology. *S.E. 1*.
Green, A. (1980). Passions et destins des passions. *Nouvelle Revue de Psychanalyse*, 21. Also in: *On Private Madness*. London: Hogarth Press, 1986.
Green, A. (1989). Préface. In: B. Brusset, *La psychanalyse du lien*. Paris: Le Centurion.
Green, A. (1995). Has sexuality anything to do with psychoanalysis? *International Journal of Psychoanalysis, 76* (5): 871.
Green, A. (1997). *Les chaînes d'éros*. Paris: Odile Jacob.
Gutton, P. (1991). *Le pubertaire*. Paris: Presses Universitaire de France.
Israël, P. (1999). L'identité brouillée du psychanalyste. *Revue Française de Psychanalyse, 63* (4): 1265–1280.
Jacquey, X. (1975). Subjectal, transitionnel, objectal. Structure des espaces imaginaires et construction de l'espace analytique. In: *Confrontations Critiques du IVème groupe*, January 1976.
Kernberg, O. (1988). Projection and projective identification: Developmental and clinical aspects. In: J. Sandler (Ed.), *Projection, Identification, Projective Identification*. London: Karnac.
Kernberg, O. (1997). *Les troubles limites de la personnalité*. Paris: Dunod.
Klein, M. (1946). *Envy and Gratitude and Other Works* (pp. 141–175). London: Hogarth Press, 1975.
Lacan, J. (1945). Logical time and the assertion of anticipated certainty. In: *Écrits* (pp. 161–175), trans. B. Fink. New York: W. W. Norton, 2006.

Lacan, J. (1949). The mirror stage as formative of the *I* function as revealed in psychoanalytic experience. In: *Écrits* (pp. 75–81), trans. B. Fink. New York: W. W. Norton, 2006.

Lacan J. (1954–55). *Séminaire II, Le moi*. Paris: Seuil, 1966.

Lacan, J. (1955–56). *Séminaire III, Les psychoses*. Paris: Seuil, 1966.

Lacan, J. (1958). The signification of the phallus. In: *Écrits* (pp. 575–584), trans. B. Fink. New York: W. W. Norton, 2006.

Lacan, J. (1959). In memory of Ernest Jones: On his theory of symbolism. In: *Écrits* (pp. 585–601), trans. B. Fink. New York: W. W. Norton, 2006.

Lacan, J. (1959–60). *Séminaire VII, L'éthique de la psychanalyse* (pp. 126–137). Paris: Seuil, 1966.

Lacan, J. (1960a). Remarks on Daniel Lagache's presentation: "Psychoanalysis and personality structure". In: *Écrits* (pp. 543–574), trans. B. Fink. New York: W. W. Norton, 2006.

Lacan, J. (1960b). The subversion of the subject and the dialectic of desire in the Freudian unconscious. In: *Écrits* (pp. 671–702), trans. B. Fink. New York: W. W. Norton, 2006.

Lacan, J. (1964). Seminar XI: The partial drive and its circuit. In: *The Four Fundamental Concepts of Psychoanalysis*. London: Hogarth Press, 1977.

Lacan, J. (1966). *Écrits*. Paris: Seuil. [English translation, *Écrits*, trans. B. Fink. New York; W. W. Norton, 2006.]

Lacan, J. (1969–70). *Séminaire XVII: L'envers de la psychanalyse*. Paris: Seuil.

Lacan, J. (2006). *Écrits*, trans. B. Fink. New York: W. W. Norton.

Lafond, C. (1999). A la recherche de la part perdue. *Revue Française de Psychanalyse, 63* (5, special issue): 1619.

Laplanche, J. (1970). *Vie et mort en Psychanalyse*. Paris: Flammarion. [*Life and Death in Psychoanalysis*, trans. J. Mehlman. Baltimore, MD: Johns Hopkins University Press, 1976.]

Laplanche, J. (1989). *New Foundations for Psychoanalysis*. Cambridge: Basil Blackwell.

Laplanche, J. (1998). La soi-disant pulsion de mort. Une pulsion sexuelle. *Adolescence, 30*: 205–225.

Laplanche, J., & Pontalis, F.-B. (1973). *The Language of Psychoanalysis*. London: Karnac, 1988.

Laufer, M., & Laufer, E. (1997). *Adolescence and Developmental Breakdown: A Psychoanalytic View*. New Haven, CT: Yale University Press.

Laznik-Penot, M. C. (1990). La mise en place du concept de jouissance chez Lacan. *Revue Française de Psychanalyse, 54* (1): 55.
Laznik-Penot, M. C. (1993). Pour une théorie lacanienne des pulsions. *Le Discours Psychanalytique, 10*: 221.
Le Gaufey, G. (1991). *L'incomplétude du symbolique*. Paris: EPEL.
Le Guen, C. (2001). Quelque chose manque. . . . De la répression aux représentations motrices. *Revue Française de Psychanalyse, 65* (1): 37–70.
Leibowitz, Y. (1987). *Science et valeurs*, trans. G. Haddad (from Hebrew). Paris: Desclée de Brouwer, Collection Midrash, 1997.
Mauger, J., & Monette, L. (2000). Pure culture [Rapport pour le Soixantième Congrès des Psychanalystes de Langue Française, Montréal]. *Revue Française de Psychanalyse, 64* (5, special issue): 1391–1400.
Neyraut, M. (1974). *Le transfert*. Paris: Presses Universitaire de France.
Penot, B. (1989). *Figures du déni—en deçà du négatif*. Paris: Dunod.
Penot, B. (1991). La psychose subjectivée. *Adolescence, 9* (2): 217–234.
Penot, B. (1993). Le narcissisme originaire à l'épreuve de l'adolescence. *Journal de la Psychanalyse de l'Enfant, 13*: 271.
Penot, B. (1995). L'instance du surmoi dans les Ecrits de J. Lacan. In: *Monographies de la Revue Française de Psychanalyse (Surmoi II)*. Paris: Presses Universitaire de France.
Penot, B. (1996). Le fantôme du désir paternel. Effet trans-générationnel et abolition symbolique. In: *Monographies de la Revue Française de Psychanalyse (Scènes originaires)*. Paris: Presses Universitaire de France.
Penot, B. (1998). Disavowal of reality as an act of filial piety. *International Journal of Psychoanalysis, 79* (1): 27.
Penot, B. (1999a). Le passion du sujet. *Revue Française de Psychanalyse, 63* (5, special issue): 1489–1561.
Penot, B. (1999b). Préface [Colloque de l'Institut du monde arabe:]. In: Z. Benchemsi, J. Fortineau, & R. Beauroy (Eds.), *La figure de l'autre, l'étranger, en psychopathologie clinique. Psychanalyse et civilisations.* Paris: L'Harmattan.
Penot, B. (2001). The drive circuit as generator of subjectivation. *International Journal of Psychoanalysis, 82* (3): 501.
Penot, B. (2005). Psychoanalytic teamwork in a day hospital—revisiting some preconditions for patients' subjective appropriation. *International Journal of Psychoanalysis, 86*: 503–515.
Perron-Borelli, M. (1997). *Dynamique du fantasme*. Paris: Presses Universitaire de France, Le fil rouge.

Poincaré, H. (1905). *La valeur de la science*. Paris: Flammarion, 1970.
Porge, E. (1989). *Se compter trois*. Toulouse: Erès, Collection Littoral.
Racamier, P.-C. (1995). *L'inceste et l'incestuel*. Paris: College de Psychanalyse.
Rassial, J.-J. (1990). *L'adolescent et le psychanalyste*. Paris: Rivages.
Rassial, J.-J. (1997). *Le sujet en état limite*. Paris: Denoël.
Renik, O. (1998). The analyst's subjectivity and the analyst's objectivity. *International Journal of Psychoanalysis, 79* (3): 487.
Renik, O. (2000). Affective self-disclosure by the analyst. *International Journal of Psychoanalysis, 81*: 164–165.
Rosenberg, B. (1991). *Masochisme mortifère et masochisme gardien de la vie*. Monographies de la Revue Française de Psychanalyse. Paris: Presses Universitaire de France.
Roussillon, R. (1995). La métapsychologie des processus. *Revue Française de Psychanalyse, 59* (5, special issue).
Schaeffer, J. (1997). *Le refus du féminin*. Paris: Presses Universitaire de France, Epîtres.
Smadja, C. (1998). Le fonctionnement opératoire dans la pratique psychosomatique. *Revue Française de Psychanalyse, 62* (5, special issue): 1367–1441.
Szwec, G. (1998). *Les galériens volontaires*. Paris: Presses Universitaire de France.
Urtubey, L. de (1994). Travail de contre-transfert. *Revue Française de Psychanalyse, 58* (5, special issue): 1271.
Widlöcher, D. (1999). Le montage pulsionnel. Ouverture et perplexités. *Revue Française de Psychanalyse, 63* (5, special issue): 1671–1678.
Winnicott, D. W. (1963). Dependence in infant-care, in child-care, and in the psycho-analytic setting. *International Journal of Psychoanalysis, 44*: 339–344. [Also in: *The Maturational Processes and the Facilitating Environment*. London: Hogarth Press, 1965; reprinted London: Karnac, 1990.]
Winnicott, D. W. (1971a). Creativity and its origins. In: *Playing and Reality* (pp. 65–85). London: Tavistock/Routledge.
Winnicott, D. W. (1971b). Mirror-role of mother and family in child development. In: *Playing and Reality* (pp. 111–119). London: Tavistock/Routledge.

INDEX

absence:
  bad subject of (clinical example: "Antonio"), 160–165
  disavowal of, and invalidation of signification, 94–97
  and symbolization, 91
abuse, incestuous, 128
academic phobia, 51
acted scansion, 165–167
acting out, 160–164
adolescence, 7, 30, 56, 79, 106–109, 116, 121, 128, 129
  entry into, of Freudian subject, 59–74
aim-presentation(s) [*Zielvorstellung*], 90, 92
Alcibiades, 128
Alexander the Great, 128
alienation, 7, 8, 41, 51, 83, 123, 140
alimentary need, 21, 29, 31
Allen, W., 129
Alquié, F., 151
amnesia, 163
"Angel" (clinical example: effect of parents' narcissistic wounds), 79–82, 105, 116
"Anna" (clinical example: capacities for sublimation), 117–122

Anna O (Bertha Pappenheim), 119, 134, 135
anorexia, 21, 24, 33, 68, 119
"Antonio" (clinical example: bad subject of absence), 160, 161, 163, 164
Anzieu, D., 60
aphasia, 70
Arfouilloux, J.-C., 76, 91
Aristotle, 88–91
art, 69, 128
  modern, 115
Artemis of the Ephesians, 49
autism, 22, 66
auto-eroticism/auto-erotic phase, 16, 19, 21, 22, 24, 29, 31, 48, 126, 155
avowal, 49, 96

Bachelard, G., 151
Balier, C., 116
Bataille, G., 151
Baudelaire, C., 128
behavioural pathologies, 52
Bergeret, J., 126, 128
binding [*Bindung*], 57, 65, 113, 125
  libidinal, 123
  psychic, 8, 73, 76, 127
Bion, W. R., 78

INDEX

Bizet, G., 119
Blos, P., 74
body image, 115, 123
Borch-Jacobsen, 91, 134, 139
borderline states, 12, 51, 164, 165, 168
   treatment of, 126–129
Botella, C., 129
Botella, S., 129
Braque, G., 151
Braunschweig, D., 124
bulimia, 12, 21, 24, 27
   (clinical example: "Vera"), 29–41

Cahn, R., 11, 61, 139
capacity for being alone, 121
castration, 95, 101, 104, 154
   complex, 96, 155
   of mother, 94
   signification of, 94
causality, 88, 90
   deductive, 89
   synchronic, 155
cause(s), four orders of, 88
   efficient, 89, 90
   final, 89, 90, 91
   formal, 89, 90
   material, 88
Cavafy, C. P., 20
"Celeste" (clinical example: family myth), 66–74
Chabert, C., 121
Char, R., 151
Chasseguet-Smirgel, J., 129
childhood psychosis, 66
Coluche (M. G. J. Colucci), 13
complexes, unconscious, 2
condensation, 2, 72, 111, 158
conditioning, 87, 147
conduct disorders, 8, 53
constructions in analysis, 81
containing speech matrix, 72
countertransference, 77, 127, 141
creativity, 3, 10, 103, 119, 121

Damourette, J., 62
death drive, 105, 112, 125, 126, 130, 148, 157, 158
   role of, 122–124
defence(s):
   narcissistic, 10, 83, 84, 163
   neurotic, 40
deferred action [après-coup, Nachträglichkeit], 12, 82, 154

delinquent drive activity, 116–117
delusion, 64, 65, 73, 76, 92
de Mijolla, A., 105, 149
Denis, P., 123, 124
depersonalization, 79
depression, 67
depressive position, 113
Descartes, R., 8, 87, 166
determinism, 82, 139, 140, 143, 168
   psychic, 51, 90, 142
   subjective, 86, 90
   synchronous, 157
   unconscious, 3
Diatkine, G., 111
Diatkine, R., 110
Diogenes, 104
disavowal [*Verleugnung*], 6, 18, 49, 58, 66, 73, 76–83, 85, 92, 96, 100, 103
   of absence, 163
   community of, 27, 140
   parental, 141
   of reality, 94
   transference of, 78
"dis-completeness", 49
dis-completing of parental other, necessary, 49
discontinuity, 12, 157, 158
discourse, 4, 51–57, 66, 68, 71, 84, 87, 90, 94, 135
   academic, 145
   of analyst, 145
   of hysteric, 145
   of master, 145
   matrix, 73
   mutual, 52
   mythic, 57, 66, 71, 73
displacement [*Übertragung*], 4, 75, 130, 158
disqualification, 80
dissociation drive, 123, 125
Donnet, J.-L., 2, 138
Dora, 134
dreamwork, 2, 158
drive(s) (*passim*):
   activity, 29, 31, 61–63, 110, 113, 125, 126, 135–137, 148, 150
   delinquent, 116–117
   circuit, as generator of subjectivation, 15–28
   concept of, 107, 115, 146
   destinies, 42, 107
   duality, 124
   id of, 123

interaction, 11, 58, 85, 116, 139, 155, 156
Other of, 22–24
passivation, 18, 21, 126
satisfaction, 48, 93, 106, 108, 117, 122–124, 148, 155
sexual, 91, 109
solutions, 122
subject, 12, 46, 49, 135–138, 142, 144
unexpected, in session, 131–149
in fantasy, implication of, 46–48
unbinding, 125
Dylan, E., 169

ego, 2, 25, 26, 47, 64, 78, 109, 129, 132, 139, 140, 147, 167
apparatus of, 123
beyond, 123
collective, 63
conscious, 8, 15
corporeal, 9, 108, 137
defences, 11, 46, 138
development, 151
"ego ideal", 99, 108, 110–113, 121
-to-ego representations, 135, 138, 144, 146
force, 107
functions of, 8
narcissistic-defensive, 108
repressive, 128
"ideal ego", 62, 108, 111–113, 121
ideal of, 62
imaginary wall of, 137–138
integration of, 27
-machine, 22
narcissistic, 3, 136, 138
nascent, 49
passive, 17
psychology, 105
repression by, 45
-skin [*moi-peau*], 60
structuring of, imaginary, 114
and subject, functional duality of, 122
therapies, 3
elsewhere within, 2–6
Eluard, P., 151
empathy, 146
empty speech, 57
Eros [life drive], 123, 125, 130
ethics, psychoanalyst's, 129, 140–142, 145–147, 166
evenly suspended attention, 132
exhibitionism, 17, 21

Fain, M., 27, 124, 140
false self, 6, 19, 124
family myth (clinical example: "Celeste"), 66–74
fantasy(ies):
construction of, 12, 46–48
formula for, 47, 141
lack of, 41
narcissistic, 48, 49
originary, 50
projection, 77
subjectivation of, three stages of, 42–50
subjective, 116
Fante, J., 161, 169
Faure, S., 13
Ferenczi, S., 26
figurability, 27
Fine, A., 13
freedom, 139–140
Freud, A., 43, 60
Freud, S. (*passim*):
"Analysis of a Phobia in a Five-Year-Old Boy", 96
Beyond the Pleasure Principle, 10, 108, 123, 125, 138, 157, 158
"Child is Being Beaten, A", 12, 42, 44, 75
three stages of subjectivation of fantasy, 42–50
Civilization and Its Discontents, 109, 122
"Constructions in Analysis", 11, 76, 81, 91
development of psychoanalytic theory of, 1–2, 4
"Economic Problem of Masochism, The", 17, 19, 123
Ego and the Id, The, 9
Group Psychology and the Analysis of the Ego, 74, 79, 109
"History of an Infantile Neurosis, From the", 80, 154
"Instincts and Their Vicissitudes", 6, 8, 12, 40, 42, 45, 46, 62, 83, 107, 108, 114, 155, 169
use of term "subject" in, 15–28
Interpretation of Dreams, The, 2, 92, 94, 131, 138
Jokes and Their Relation to the Unconscious, 149
"Narcissism: An Introduction, On", 9, 48, 65, 109

Freud, S. (*continued*):
"Negation", 9, 83
"Neurosis and Psychosis", 64
"Notes upon a Case of Obsessional Neurosis", 149
"Observations on Transference-Love", 142, 143
patients:
Anna O (Bertha Pappenheim), 119, 134, 135
Dora, 134
Little Hans, 96
Rat Man, 149
Wolf Man, 46, 48, 80
"Project for a Scientific Psychology", 19, 92
"Psycho-analytic Notes on an Autobiographical Account of a Case of Paranoia (Dementia paranoides)", 24, 47
"Psychogenesis of a Case of Homosexuality in a Woman, The", 97, 98
"Remembering, Repeating and Working-Through", 166
"Repression", 108
"Sexual Theories of Children, On the", 93
"Some Psychical Consequences of the Anatomical Distinction Between the Sexes", 103
Studies on Hysteria, 129
"Uncanny, The", 4
"Unconscious, The", 108
fusion, 100, 125, 158

gender, other, perception of, 4
Gilbert's disease, 79
good and evil, concepts of, 88
Green, A., 6, 15, 18, 126, 127
Gutton, P., 59, 74
Guyomard, P., 165

hallucination, 46, 65, 92
Hamlet, 61
Heraclitus, 125
homosexuality, 27, 74, 96
female (clinical example: "Nicole"), 97–105, 107, 140
human sciences, 88, 90
hyperactivity, 166
compulsive, 25
hypnotism/hypnosis, 92, 145

"I" [*ich*], 43
complexity of, 9–11
id [*Es*], 9, 10, 13, 83, 137, 145, 148
of drive, 123
ideal ego, 62, 108, 111–113, 121
idealism, 95
idealization, 100, 112
place of, 108–109
identification(s), 9, 39, 57, 110, 123, 140
imaginary, 62
mutual, 77
narcissistic, 120
projective, 78, 79
imaginary, 9, 10, 89, 114, 137–141, 144, 150, 155
category of, 87, 157
imaginary formations, 108
imaginary register, 122, 140
incestuous abuse, 128
infantile neurosis, 60
infantile sexuality, 94
inhibition(s), 72, 126, 128
insomnia, 66
inspiration, creative, 3, 123, 139
intentionality, 89
internal imago, paternal, 121
International Psychoanalytical Association, 146, 165
interpretation(s), 26, 70, 83, 127, 132
intersubjectivity, 164
introjection, 110, 112, 121
Israël, P., 169

Jacquey, X., 92
Jones, E., 95
Joseph, B., 78
Jullian, M.-E., 13
Jung, C. G., 4

Kandinsky, W., 151
Kernberg, O., 126, 127
Klein, M., 78, 113

Lacan, J. (*passim*):
drive circuit, 20–28
Ecrits, 151, 154
Ego in Freud's Theory and in the Technique of Psychoanalysis, The, 136
Ethics of Psychoanalysis, The, 1, 114, 115, 145
"Logical Time and the Assertion of Anticipated Certainty", 150, 151

"Logic of Fantasy, The", 8, 166
L schema, 136–139, 167
"Memory of Ernest Jones: On his Theory of Symbolism, In", 52
"Mirror Stage as Formative of the *I* Function as Revealed in Psychoanalytic Experience, The", 25, 150, 151
mirror stage, 25, 26, 150
"Other Side of Psychoanalysis, The", 87, 144
"Partial Drive and Its Circuit, The", 20, 94
paternal metaphor, 4
reliance of on linguistics, 7
"Remarks on Daniel Lagache's Presentation: 'Psychoanalysis and Personality Structure'", 108
"Subversion of the Subject and the Dialectic of Desire in the Freudian Unconscious, The, 85, 157
see also imaginary; real; signifier; symbolic
Lafond, C., 139, 140, 149
Lagache, D., 108
Lamartine, A. de, 48
language(s), 2, 12, 22, 85, 95, 154
   mathematical, 87
Laplanche, J., 22, 92, 114, 125
latency, 63, 104, 106, 107, 129
   and subjectivation and sublimation, 106–130
Laufer, E., 60
Laufer, M., 60
Laznik-Penot, M. C., 11, 22, 109
Le Gaufey, G., 5
Le Guen, C., 47
Leibowitz, Y., 88, 147
libidinal motor, 24–27
libido, 25, 29, 109, 113
   narcissistic, 124
life drive [*Eros*], 123, 125, 130
"*little a*", 22, 47, 122, 144
Little Hans, 96
love–hate of transference, 142–144
"L" schema (Lacan), 136–139, 167

Magritte, R., 95, 115
Maïmonides, 88
masochism, 24, 109, 123
   primary, 17, 19
masochistic phase, 16

masturbation, 106
maternal phobia, 26
Matisse, H., 151
Mauger, J., 111
mentalization, problems of, familial, 65–74
metapsychology, 2, 3, 8, 12, 15, 108, 122, 139
   second, 123, 158
mirror stage, 25, 26, 150
miscarriage, 39
Moebius strip, 166
Monette, L., 111
mother:
   castration of, 94
   "dis-completeness" of, 49
   phallic, 49
mourning, 66, 70, 90, 99
   unachieved, 65
M'Uzan, M. de, 129
myth, family (clinical example: "Celeste", 66–74)
mythic speech/discourse, 57, 66, 71, 73

narcissism, 9, 10, 48, 60, 64, 66, 125
   primary, 24
narcissistic container, 61
narcissistic defence(s), 10, 58, 66, 83, 84, 112, 163
narcissistic fantasy, primary, 48–49
narcissistic ideal, 109, 112
narcissistic seduction, 54
natural sciences, 86, 89, 90
neuroleptics, 68
neurosis(es):
   infantile, 60
   obsessional, 8
neurotic defences, 40
neurotic symptoms, 94, 110, 126, 158
Neyraut, M., 141
"Nicole" (clinical example: female homosexuality), 97–105, 107, 140
object:
   of drive, 47, 107, 114
   use of term in psychoanalysis, 47, 114
"*object a*", 47, 113, 122, 145
obsessional neuroses, 8
oedipal period, 106
Oedipus complex (clinical example: South American patient), 159–160
"operation meta", 2
oral dependence, 21, 31

oral drive functioning and subjection
(clinical example: "Vera"), 29–41
Other of drive, 22–24

Pappenheim, B. (Anna O), 119, 134, 135
paralysis, 70, 72
paranoid delusions, 117
paraphrenics, 65
parapraxis, 120
parental detachment, 124
parental imagos, 60
parental investment, 25
good, role of, 124–126
parental other, 23, 46, 58, 96, 116, 140, 148
dis-completing of, 49
Paris Psychoanalytical Society, 62, 165
Paris Psychosomatic School, 25
Parkinson's disease, 98
Pasolini, P. P., 80
passivation, 17, 23, 25, 29, 30, 107, 123, 125, 136, 140, 148, 149, 155
analyst's acceptance of, 39, 97, 144, 163, 165
and the construction of fantasy, 12, 42–50
drive, 18, 21, 126
oral, 21
mutual, 29, 116
oral, 21
vs. passivity, 6–7, 18
phase of, 148
of psychoanalyst subject, 167–169
reciprocal, 11, 166
subjectivating, 10
passivity, 11, 17, 25, 29, 30, 68, 166
vs. passivation, 6–7, 18
paternal metaphor, 4, 105, 130
penis envy, 26
Penn, S., 129
Penot, B., 9, 13, 18, 49, 61, 64, 65, 76, 77, 86, 92, 163, 169
perceptive memories vs. fantasy, 44
Perron-Borelli, M., 46
perverse position, 25, 129
perversions, 16, 17, 42, 43, 115, 126
phallic mother, 49
phallic phase, 94
phallus, 12, 91
paternal, 98
signifier, and subjectivation of sexuality, 93–105

phobia, 51, 96
maternal, 26
school, 117
Picasso, P., 151
Pichon, E., 62
Plato, myth of cave, 2
pleasure principle, 11, 139, 143
beyond, 10, 108, 123, 124
Poincaré, H., 88
Ponge, F., 151
Pontalis, F.-B., 92
Porge, E., 158, 169
Pragier, G., 13, 43
primal helplessness [*Hilflosigkeit*], 25
primal scene, 48
primary narcissism, 24
primary narcissistic fantasy, 48–49
primary thought process, 2, 95
projection, 77, 78, 83
projective identification, 78, 79
proto-identification with father, 74
proto-subject, exterior, 83
psychic apparatus, 1, 4, 8, 10, 15, 48, 75, 106, 136, 138, 145, 146
structural heterogeneity of, 2
psychic category, the real as, 75
psychic functioning, determinism of, 90
psychic pain, 65
psychic real/reality, 27, 46, 62, 64, 65, 138, 141, 155
transference of, 82–84
psychic register(s), 112, 157
psychoanalysis, other side of, 144–148
psychoanalyst, ethics of, 140–142
psychoanalytic institutes, 90
psychodrama, 77, 110, 168
psychopathic behaviours, 116
psychosis, 8, 26, 61, 64, 65, 71, 79, 86, 92, 117
childhood, 53, 66
psychotic symptoms, 64
puberty, 31, 59–61, 64, 106, 107, 117

Queneau, R., 151

Racamier, P.-C., 55
Rassial, J.-J., 60, 127
Rat Man, 149
real, as psychic category, 10, 75
register:
imaginary, 10, 156
real, 10, 156
symbolic, 10, 156, 157

regression, 26
  formal, 92
Renik, O., 28, 92
reparation(s), 25, 162
repetition:
  compulsion [*Wiederholungszwang*], 82, 83, 143, 157, 162, 168
  induced in the other, 76, 77
repressed, return of, 110, 163
repression, 45, 73, 109, 111, 126, 168
  original, 114
  of sexuality, 110
resistance, 3, 140
restitution [*Wiederherstellung*], 76, 91
return of the repressed, 110, 163
Rosenberg, B., 109
Rosenfeld, H., 78
Rouault, G., 151
Roussillon, R., 123, 158
Roustang, F., 92

sadism, 16, 19, 24, 45
  original, 17
sadomasochistic drives, 16
sadomasochistic phase, 16
scansion(s), 12, 152, 164
  acted, 165–167
  signifying, 154, 156–158
  suspensive, 153
  temporal, 150, 154
Schaeffer, J., 10
schizophrenia, 79
Schreber, D. G. M., 47
scientificity, and psychoanalytic approach, 86–91
scientific objectivity, 90
scopophilia, 17
self-knowledge, 154
sexual differentiation, 5, 61, 62
sexuality, subjectivation of, and phallus signifier, 93–105
significance, 158
signification, 23, 27, 40, 131, 150, 155
  of castration, 94
  foreclosure of, and suffering subject, 75–92
  invalidation of, and disavowal of absence, 94–97
  suspension of, 164
signifier(s), 22, 23, 79, 129, 134, 138, 148, 149, 156, 157
  conceptualization of, 12, 84–86, 91, 133
  direct, 135–136
  foreclosure of, 78
  fundamental tool of Lacanian theory, 122
  Lacanian definition of, 96
  little a as corollary of, 122
  phallus signifier, and subjectivation of sexuality, 93–105
  role of, 141, 166
  and subjective, 86
  toponymic, 84
  verbal, 104, 105, 135
signifying chains, 137
signifying imprint, 23
signifying scansion(s), 154, 156–158
slip of tongue, 38
Smadja, C., 8, 130
"Sophie" (clinical example: bad subject), 23, 51–58, 116
splitting(s) [*schize*], 66, 77, 80
Strachey, J., 16, 18, 28, 91, 92, 146
subject(s) (*passim*):
  "bad", 51, 52, 58
  of absence, 160–165
  to come (clinical example: "Sophie"), 51–58
  conceptualization of, 6–7, 12
  drive, 12, 46, 49
  in fantasy, implication of, 46–48
  unexpected, in session, 131–149
  extraneous, 16, 17
  Freudian, 18
  adolescence of, 59–74
  function, 6, 7, 10–12, 22, 58, 59, 63, 108, 123, 128, 138, 139, 148
  in L schema, 137
  manifest and latent-absent, 158–159
  "new", 8, 16, 17, 19, 22, 62, 83, 107, 132
  psychoanalyst, passivation of, 167–169
  suffering, 164
  and foreclosure of signification, 75–92
  "supposed to know", 144
  use of term in Freud's *Instincts and Their Vicissitudes*, 15–28
subjection, 6, 61
  alienating, 39
  and oral drive functioning (clinical example: "Vera"), 29–41
  vs. subjectivation, 18, 24, 30
  transference of, 40

subjectivation, 11, 30, 37, 40, 41, 105, 136, 140, 142, 148
  clinical work with, 7–9
  disorders of, 12, 75–92, 138
    in adolescence, 7, 51–58, 59–74
  drive circuit as generator of, 15–28
  of fantasy, three stages of, 42–50
  logical stages of, 150–170
  masochistic, 45
  vs. subjection, 6
  and sublimation, and latency, 106–130
subjectivity, 6, 12, 15, 23, 85–87, 90, 135, 139, 162
  human, precarious position of, 1
sublimation, 12, 47, 63, 105, 149
  definition, 114
  drive, 110
  and subjectivation, and latency, 106–130
sublimatory activity, 113–116
sublimatory libidinal investments, 121
sublimatory quest, object of, 113–115
sublimatory solution, 110–113
suicide attempt, 120
superego, 9, 26, 64, 110, 113, 163
  paternal, 111
  repressive, 111
surrealist movement, 115
symbiosis, 24
symbolic, 10
  incompleteness of, 5
symbolic equation, 130
symbolic operator(s), 59, 108, 112
symbolic register, 122, 156
symbolization, 53, 65, 74, 75, 92, 113, 114, 116, 122, 144
  and absence, 91
  capacity for, 72
    deficiency in, 73
  primary, 164
synchronic causality, 155
synchronous determinism, 157
Szwec, G., 25

"talking cure", 129, 135
teamwork, psychoanalytic, 77–81, 168
telepathy, 79
temporal scansion, 150, 154
thing-representation(s), 2, 82, 94, 95, 104, 115, 158
thought, mode of, operative, 8
time and space, relation between, 151

transference, 52, 60, 76, 107, 125, 126, 133, 145, 146, 166
  actualization, 77
  alienated, 40, 83
  analyst's involvement in, 127
  in clinical example:
    "Antonio", 161, 164
    "Nicole", 101, 105
    "Vera", 27, 30–32, 39
  concept of, 156, 168
  and countertransference, 77, 127, 141
  of disavowal, 78
  erotic, 143
  and failure of adolescent process, 60, 107
  fantasy, 75, 141
  love–hate of, 142–144
  negative, 127
  object, 75
  paternal, 125
  phenomenon(a), 27
  of psychic real, 82–84
  regressive, 40
  relationship, 21, 26, 27
  of subjection, 40
transitional function, 73
transitional space, 52
troubadour repertoire, 115
true and false, concepts of, 88
truthfulness, 143

unbinding, 49, 105, 125, 148, 157
uncanny, 66, 77, 84, 86
Unconscious [*Ucs*], 2, 8, 94, 95, 129, 131, 137, 146, 168
unconscious complexes, 2
unlinking, subjective, 158
Urtubey, L. de, 83

"Vera" (clinical example: bulimia/oral drive functioning and subjection), 21, 27, 29–41, 49, 104, 140, 166
Villon, F., 128

Widlöcher, D., 86
"wild children", 23
Winnicott, D. W., 26, 27, 52, 76, 83, 121, 124, 151, 163
Wolf Man, 46, 48, 80
working through [*perlaboration, Durcharbeitung*], 5, 8, 31, 77, 83, 159